WHY OUR KIDS DON'T STUDY

WHY OUR KIDS DON'T STUDY

An Economist's Perspective

John D. Owen

The Johns Hopkins University Press

Baltimore and London

© 1995 The Johns Hopkins University Press
All rights reserved. Published 1995
Printed in the United States of America on acid-
free paper
04 03 02 01 00 99 98 97 96 95   5 4 3 2 1

The Johns Hopkins University Press
2715 North Charles Street
Baltimore, Maryland 21218-4319
The Johns Hopkins Press Ltd., London

ISBN 0-8018-4925-X

Library of Congress Cataloging-in-Publication Data
will be found at the end of this book.
A catalog record for this book is available from the
British Library.

Contents

Preface

In writing this book, I have used the tools of labor economics to analyze shortfalls in student achievement. Labor economics, or, more broadly, the economics of human resources, has in the last thirty-odd years come to include such diverse subjects as racial and gender discrimination, fertility, marriage, housework, crime, health care, and recreational activities. Education and training were early examples: the human capital revolution inaugurated in the early 1960s focused on decisions to keep young people in schools or in training, in the expectation that they would become more productive adults. Economists, however, have largely ignored another dimension of the economics of schooling: the effort of young people while in school—the amount of work they do, inside and outside class, which is directed to learning. Yet this is a critically important factor in our economic success or failure today.

I have long thought that student effort provides a fruitful application of labor economics. We know that variations in this effort determine how effective outlays on education will be in raising the skill level of the nation's work force. It seems reasonable to ask whether the level of student effort can be analyzed as a form of labor supply.

These two topics—the labor-leisure choice and the economics of education—have been my principal research interests for a long time. To analyze student effort, however, I have also considered what the sociologists have to say about how our educational institutions fail to encourage hard work as well as what the psychologists tell us about why students dislike study. (Members of the psychology department at Wayne State University were especially helpful to me at this stage.) Recent work by economists about how poorly the labor market rewards young employees for their academic achievement has filled in another part of the puzzle.

This emphasis on the factors that influence the incentives of young people to supply study effort helps to bridge the fields of labor economics and education reform. Much labor supply analysis today consists of discerning the effects of complex institutional incentives (such as those provided by our system of taxes and transfer payments) on the supply of work to the market. Most educational reformers, in effect, offer ways of increasing incentives to study.

In presenting this work, I have endeavored to break with the common tradition among economists and have eschewed all mathematical analysis; there are no tables or graphs in the text. The few technical terms used are explained in full. The issues discussed here are too pressing to be restricted to an "economists-only" audience.

I would like to thank my colleagues in the economics and psychology departments and in the College of Urban, Labor, and Metropolitan Affairs at Wayne State University as well as those at other universities, especially Jacob Mincer of Columbia University, Michael Podgursky at the University of Massachusetts at Amherst, and Alan Sorkin at the University of Maryland at Baltimore County, for helpful comments on earlier drafts. I also owe a debt to the economics department and to the College of Urban, Labor, and Metropolitan Affairs at Wayne State University for their generous financial support of this project.

My wife, Jean, knows that her support and editorial advice were crucial at several stages in researching and writing the book.

Introduction

Since the publication of *A Nation at Risk* in 1983, most Americans have agreed that our education system badly needs reform. That report of the National Commission on Excellence in Education revealed the sorry state of education in the United States, the social damage poor schooling does, and the need for change. For the next decade books, articles, reports, and congressional hearings discussed educational reform, while public dissatisfaction with the system remained undiminished.

This book focuses on the student, specifically, on student "effort"— days of school attended per year and hours spent in the classroom or doing homework—along with more subtle measures, such as the level of seriousness of the curriculum or the percentage of class time teachers use for teaching.

Much of the literature on reforming the kindergarten-to-twelfth-grade (K–12) system undervalues the role of students in supplying study effort. This book draws on economics and other social science disciplines to assess the critical role of student effort in our prosperity and proffers practicable strategies for raising it above its current mediocre levels.

We know that the low level of effort of American students in the K–12 system is a major cause of their poor achievement and that turning this situation around is essential if we are to reform education and provide a work force and a citizenry that is prepared to rise to the opportunities the new century will bring.

When we *do* ask ourselves why effort is so low, we raise other interesting issues: Why do school system rules demand so little effort from students? Why are students themselves so poorly motivated to do homework or pay attention in class? We will see that levels of student effort have roots in more basic issues, such as how schools themselves are structured and how they interface with labor markets.

Keeping our focus on student effort allows us to relate a key education issue to a well-developed economic concept: the theory of labor supply. For twenty years analysts have studied how labor supply reacts to incentives as broad as changes in all workers' hourly wages and as narrow as shifts in particular income-support programs. Labor supply theory can, and does, shed light on phenomena as diverse as working males' declining working hours, the increase in the number of employed women, and the popularity of early retirement. The concept can also be applied to narrower topics, such as labor's response to government income-maintenance schemes and to private or government pension plans.

Applying labor supply theory to the supply of student effort lets us discuss the differences between students and others. To those who argue that study is not at all the same as work, that some people find it very pleasant, empirical researchers might reply that the average young person finds both study and paid work intrinsically unpleasant and prefers to occupy his or her time in other ways. Many adult employees feel the same way, yet both adults and students can be induced to work by a system of rewards and punishments. The differences between adult workers and students can be explained by the different reward systems available to the two groups: young people are not as well rewarded for studying as employees are for working, and they respond accordingly. As for punishments, imposing heavier workloads on students would, in principle, raise effort; in practice, however, giving students more work without substantially improving their rewards would increase the dropout rate and lead to other unacceptable social fallout.

Why not improve rewards?[1] School governance and interaction with the labor market dictate the reward system. Bringing student incentives closer to the adult level would mean changes in the schools themselves and their relation to the labor market.

The reform literature cited here, from sociology, psychology, and education, as well as economics, focuses on grades K–12 rather than higher education, not because the problem goes away with the high school diploma—as a college teacher, I know it does not—but because here the gap between U.S. school achievement and that of our competitors is clearest.

THE SUPPLY OF STUDY EFFORT

Chapter 1
Our Kids Don't Study Much

Experts on educational systems and parents agree that American children do very little studying. Typically, school is in session only 180 days a year, fewer than half the days available. School days usually include about five hours of class time, and time actually spent teaching is limited: between students' absences from class and lack of attention while in class as well as interruptions by outsiders, about one-half of scheduled "teaching time" is lost.[1] Moreover, a good deal of teaching time consists of what classroom observers describe as "banter," exchanges between the teacher and students designed to improve the teacher's relationship with the class, rather than fostering the students' education. Finally, American students put in very little effort outside of class—an hour a day or less for high school students and even less for elementary school students.[2]

An Important Factor in Academic Achievement

When confronted with one more report of our unsatisfactory educational progress, a typical response is to ask: "What is wrong with our schools?" We then go on to criticize teachers, principals, and others who are employed in our school system. We often overlook the weakness of the schools' basic "work force": the students.

The study effort of children is a major component of the resources the nation devotes to education. Even at the present low level of effort, the hours students spend on schoolwork are many times greater than those worked by teachers and administrators combined. The somewhat shorter hours per student are outweighed by their greater numbers, relative to school system employees. Pupils in our public elementary and secondary schools outnumber teachers seventeen to one. And, though schools now employ almost as many nonteaching staff members as teachers, there are still more than nine pupils per system employee (U.S. Department of Education 1991b). The typical statistics on resources consumed by education do not highlight the contribution of this student time. The data indicate that the direct, or out-of-pocket, costs of education are very great—moving up toward half a trillion a year.[3] The value, or "opportunity cost," of this student time is also very large, especially at the high school level, when students have the physical maturity to earn a living in the labor market. Some estimates of the opportunity costs of student time put it at nearly the same level as the direct costs of education. If that were true, student time is worth hundreds of billions of dollars annually.

Students as Customers or Workers?

Some readers may regard the notion of a student work force as strange, and certainly workers differ from students in a number of ways. We might, instead, think of students as customers who purchase a service from the educational system, as suggested by David Kearns and Denis Doyle, two recent critics of the school system. While there is some logic to their position, the analogy is flawed because educational services are offered at no cost through twelfth grade and because students are required by law to consume these services until they are sixteen years old. Treating students as customers diverts attention from the special importance of student effort in education.

Education, of course, is not the only product that requires considerable client or customer effort to be consumed. Other situations include, for example, an accident victim working with a physical therapist, an overweight individual following a Weight Watchers regimen and attending aerobics classes, and a recovering alcoholic in an inpatient treatment program. In all these cases the effort of the subject—whether he or she is called a student, a patient, a client, or a customer—may determine the success or failure of the person's improvement program.

Effort is not the only important input here. A poorly designed program or lazy or incompetent treatment personnel can sabotage a client's improvement. Individual motivation, however, is the primary factor in the success of the activity.

A client's effort is nowhere more important than in school; it is critical to academic success. Most of us know from observation that lazy students do not learn very much, and empirical researchers support this commonsense view with demonstrations of the positive effects on academic achievement of completed homework assignments, a stronger curriculum, and increased "time on task" in the classroom.[4]

Of course, the school system itself plays a role in determining student achievement. Requirements set by the school help to determine the level of student effort, while the teaching provided by individual instructors can stimulate (or fail to stimulate) effort and so influence achievement (Hanushek 1986). And, of course, schools influence what students can accomplish in other ways: student effort can be wasted if pedagogy is not well designed or focuses on material that is not pertinent to long-term educational goals.[5]

Yet it is the effort of the student which is of paramount importance in determining the success of our educational system. Seen this way, comparing students to workers makes sense.

The Effects of Low Level of Study Effort

Americans today see the pervasive effects of unsatisfactory student achievement. Employers looking for literacy, numeracy, and good work habits can no longer rely on the high school diploma to guarantee these qualities. Those concerned about the nation's unfavorable balance of trade and those trying to prevent the export of well-paying skilled jobs point to the disparities in achievement between U.S. students and those in competing nations.[6]

These disparities are real. Repeated comparisons of Americans with European and Japanese youngsters show us near the bottom in achievement in mathematics, science, language, and other cognitive skills. For years defenders of the status quo tried to dismiss such findings on the ground that, while ours is a democratic, inclusive system that offers education to all U.S. citizens, other countries provide secondary school educations only to an elite group. Yet the same depressing comparisons are obtained even when only pre–high school students are examined. Moreover, rates of high school completion have risen rapidly in a number of countries, often to U.S. levels (National Center on Education and the Economy 1990, 43).

We are also familiar with the linkage between higher levels of achievement and greater study effort abroad. Comparative data on days spent in school per year, homework time, and classroom syllabi confirm our everyday observations. For example, none of our competitors schedules summer vacations as long as those American children enjoy. Japanese students spend one-third more days per year in school than students in the United States. Moreover, their absence rate is only one-third of ours, further increasing the difference in days of school attended. Compare homework done by U.S. and Japanese high school students, for example. The average American student spends less than one hour a night doing homework; only 6 percent devote more than ten hours a week to doing it, while 75 percent spend from zero to five hours on homework (Fetters, Brown, and Owings 1984). In Japan the average student puts in fifteen hours: two hours of homework each day during a six-day school week plus three hours on Sunday. This is in addition to the daily hour and a half Japanese students spend commuting in order to attend selective, often specialized, high schools (Rohlen 1983, 275).[7] Comparison with students in Western Europe also show Americans putting in less effort.

Changes over Time in Study Effort

Why has our situation worsened? Data on changes over time in student effort are extremely difficult to obtain. The data on changes in achievement are better but are far from satisfactory. Understandably, there are different assessments of the long-term trends. Many critical observers perceive a decline in study effort in the 1960s and 1970s, when curricula were diluted, less homework was assigned, and classroom discipline was relaxed (Sedlak and others 1986, 2). In the 1980s attempts to reverse this trend, largely through curriculum reform, have met only limited success.[8]

The achievement data appear to show little net change.[9] A number of writers have said that there has been a decline in student achievement, but a recent analysis contests this finding. According to R. S. Herrnstein and Charles Murray, the widely cited decline of Scholastic Aptitude Test (SAT) scores from the 1960s to 1980 was preceded by a sharp increase from the 1950s to the 1960s, so there was little net change.[10] Different definitions of achievement can also yield different interpretations of the data. For example, these authors find that while the quantitative skills of high school graduates taking the SAT tests increased, their verbal skills declined. A further difficulty is that there have been changes in the relative performance of different groups in the population. The gap between blacks and whites in reading achievement, for example, has been reduced, from about 5.3 years upon graduation from high school in the 1950s to about 2.6 years.[11] At the same time performance within the highest-ability percentiles has declined.

The experts may disagree on the extent and significance of declining achievement levels, but they agree that the economy has changed in ways that mandate much more education and that many Americans do not have the skills to obtain good jobs in the new workplace. The changing labor market is hardest on those near the bottom of the skills distribution hierarchy. Good jobs for "strong backs and weak minds" are becoming scarce. This helps to explain an apparent paradox: that youngsters from disadvantaged backgrounds who have significantly higher levels of academic achievement than their parents and who have, moreover, made some progress toward reducing the disparity between their levels of achievement and the national average are still finding it more difficult to land good jobs. In the rapidly changing market these young people have to be even better prepared simply to maintain their labor market status.

Chapter 2

Students Prefer To Do Other Things

For generations adults have noticed the aversion of young people to studying. In recent years psychologists and sociologists have undertaken systematic studies of these attitudes. Mihaly Csikszentmihalyi and Reed Larson examined middle-class students in a "very good high school" with excellent teachers.[1] The researchers employed an interesting methodology. Participating students wore pagers and carried questionnaire forms for a week. The investigators activated the pagers at random times, once in every two-hour period. The students were then asked to write down whether they enjoyed what they were doing at that time or whether they would rather be doing something else. They expressed strongly negative attitudes toward thinking, classwork, and studying. One girl assessed study time in this way: "This homework is driving me up a wall—I am just sick of it. It is boring and useless and I wish I could do something else—anything else!! I HATE HOMEWORK" (10).

But if there is agreement that American students dislike classes and homework, especially those in the middle and higher grades, there is no consensus about why they don't like it. We cannot simply assume that study is inherently unpleasant; a negative attitude could be the result of the way children are socialized.

Modern economists have had little to say about education's socialization function, concentrating instead on its role in furthering cognitive achievement. Economist Herbert Gintis is an exception; he incorporated into economic theory the notion that schools are expected to socialize children to adopt adult values as well as to teach them skills. In practice this requires that schools *change* students' values and preferences, not just endeavor to satisfy those they already possess. In this respect the education "industry" differs sharply from others. True, firms do use advertising to persuade people to buy their products. Successful firms, however, will generally try first to develop products that their customers want; if they fail to do so, advertising cannot be relied on to convince people to buy their products or services.[2] In contrast, schools are expected to change the values, and hence the preferences, of their "customers." Parents, and the larger society, demand that schools develop useful habits and build good character in the young people in their charge.

Gintis's own use of socialization theory is not directly relevant to the issue of student effort.[3] Social scientists outside the economics profession, however, have developed theories that help us to understand how the schools shape the attitudes of young people toward study and how this in turn affects the amount and quality of study effort. In recent years much of this work has been directed to explaining how our system actually has a dysfunctional effect: it encourages *negative* attitudes toward study.

Studying and Self-Esteem

A number of U.S. social scientists have accepted an ego-based theory that explains student motivation in terms of the desire to maintain and improve self-esteem.[4] This desire colors the individual's perceptions as well as his or her decisions.

According to the theory, when self-esteem is not threatened, a child can find learning to be a pleasant, exciting activity. In the early grades of elementary school, children can see learning as a way of mastering new skills. Even when they learn rather slowly, they feel pleasure that their efforts are yielding results and find that they have extended their intellectual powers. Their self-esteem is maintained or improved.[5]

As they reach the middle grades, however, children gradually move from "task involvement" to "ego involvement" in their learning. They begin to perceive learning situations as opportunities to compare themselves with others and thus discover, and demonstrate to others, that they are more or less able. Moreover, while the performance of a child is actually a result of innate ability and effort, children learn that it is the former, not the latter, which confers status in our society. Eventually, their self-esteem becomes dependent on how their ability is perceived, both by themselves and by others.[6]

Our schools reinforce this developmental tendency to regard learning progress as a measure of ability. Tests, grades, and teacher comments are all structured to provide estimates of the child's ability (Covington 1984), and for many students the result is that learning challenges diminish their self-esteem. According to the National Education Association (NEA), the practice of comparing students to the best in their class can make most students suffer a loss of self-esteem as they become sensitive to slights on their ability (Raffini 1988). If a teacher says, "This is good work; you must have worked hard on it," the student will probably feel that his or her innate ability has been devalued—that the teacher believes the youngster had to make an extra effort to achieve a satisfactory performance. According to these theorists, by the time they are ready for high school, many of our students have begun to avoid learning challenges, regarding them as unpleasant threats to their self-esteem. They seek ways to protect themselves, by, for example, picking learning challenges that are either absurdly easy or absurdly difficult, since their ego is involved in neither case. Or, when a task is assigned by the teacher rather than chosen by students, they will often respond by not applying themselves; if they don't try to succeed, they can maintain their self-esteem by telling themselves that failure does not reflect their true abilities but is, instead, the result of their weak effort (Nicholls 1984). Eventually, as students disassociate themselves from learning activities, they begin to find classes "boring." The process starts in the upper elementary grades and is fully developed by the time the student reaches high school. The result contributes to a psychological and social climate that is often quite hostile to efforts to increase achievement (see chap. 6 below).

Some social scientists are skeptical of this argument, pointing to the very weak relation between self-esteem and learning. In his interesting review of the literature, Martin Covington (1984, 78–79) points out that while

> a large number of studies over the past seventy-five years have demonstrated a positive association between self-esteem variables and academic achievement, . . . researchers have found that about 96% or 97% of the variation in achievement we observe in classrooms . . . can be explained by influences other than those traditionally associated with the notion of self-concept. . . . [Moreover,] most of these studies are correlational, and as such are of little more than circumstantial value in making a case for causation or for the direction of any causal relationship.

Such objections to the argument that self-esteem determines scholarly achievement *do not*, however, rebut the findings that students will dislike learning situations that threaten their self-esteem. Many people achieve good results while performing tasks they detest. Sometimes we find them distasteful because we know we don't perform them well—adults have egos too. But we carry on with the job as long as there are sufficient rewards and punishments to condition our actions.[7]

There are alternative explanations of the alienation of young people from their studies. John Condry (1978, 185) uses history to argue that, in the course of economic development, we have seen "a steady and unswerving increase in 'abstract' learning and a steady decrease in the learning of specific skills in a context where they are meaningful . . . a *decontextualization* of knowledge. Abstract skills are taught that are recognized to have a wide application, but these skills are taught in circumstances far removed from those where they will be used and by persons with whom the 'student' typically has little relationship." He contrasts the modern child with a male child in a hunter-gatherer society who "is aware of the consequences both to himself and to his society of his developing skill as a competent, spear-throwing hunter." Moreover, he "is able to monitor his progress in the form of play. . . . When skills are learned in context . . . the motivation for acquisition is intrinsic. . . . Skills so learned are sharpened by a desire for competence." On the other hand: "When skills are taken out of the context in which they are relevant, *motivation* then becomes a problem" (emphasis in original).

A third explanation of why students dislike studying stresses the influence of television and popular music on young people. According to this argument, continuous exposure to images of immediate gratification which require neither hard work nor significant intellectual input biases their attitudes, expectations, and habits. Even skillful teachers are hard-pressed to find material for classroom presentation (or for homework) which is as attractive to youngsters as that offered by the popular media.[8]

It can also be argued that motion pictures and television shows that present negative images of teachers and schools and caricature serious students as bookworms, or "nerds," further undermine young people's interest in study.[9] It is not clear, however, to what extent the presentation of these views in the media simply reflects student attitudes rather than determines them.

National Attitudes toward Study Effort:
Native Ability or Hard Work?

Comparisons with other countries suggest a fourth reason for the low value U.S. children place on study time: a less-than-positive attitude among adults. In Japan elites have long known that rapid educational progress is essential for the prosperity and security of their country. A positive national philosophy, as well as the institutions it has fostered, has given strong support to child-rearing practices that encourage youngsters to study. Japanese mothers begin by teaching their toddlers that effort is desirable for its own sake. They tell their children stories (not unlike our fairy tales) which make the point that "devotion to hard work itself is the mark of virtue." They then teach older preschoolers that study effort is an especially noble form of effort. In this way mothers gradually socialize their children to value study effort highly. Mothers continue to support a positive attitude toward study effort when the child begins school and maintain their support right through the child's high school years (White 1987).[10]

Japanese educational institutions themselves reinforce this emphasis on effort. The schools deemphasize individual differences in innate ability. Students who are not successful are convinced by their early training, reinforced by messages from teachers, parents, and other students, that their failure is due to insufficient effort, not a lack of ability. In Japan "potential is regarded . . . as egalitarian—everyone has it, but some work harder to develop it than others" (White 1987, 19). In contrast with the United States, individual ability is not tested in the school. Where students are tracked, or when they obtain admission to a prestigious high school, it is on the basis of the score, or grades, on *achievement* tests, not on intelligence quotient (IQ) tests or what would be a Japanese version of an SAT or American College Testing Program (ACT) exam.[11]

Present-day Japanese attitudes have some superficial similarities with those common in the United States in the nineteenth and early twentieth centuries. American educators then also believed that achievement was a result of effort, not ability. But the differences between the two systems are instructive. American teachers and school administrators in that era were imbued with the Protestant work ethic; they did not look kindly on what they considered to be lazy students and did not hesitate to impose corporal punishment on low achievers or simply expel them. Careful distinctions on the basis of ability were not possible, because of very large classes, rigid regulations, and a lack of test instruments. Moreover, with space at a premium in overcrowded public schools, it seemed reasonable to restrict access to those youngsters who applied themselves (Tyack 1974, 28–77). In time modern test instruments were developed, financing for schools became more generous, and the U.S. educational establishment adopted a more tolerant philosophy. The result was the contemporary emphasis in U.S. schools on student ability.

Other developed nations also grant a higher status to traditional learning and to study effort than is common in our country, and this contributes to a more positive attitude toward study there as well. For example, European parents have typically placed importance on good scholarship; schooling is regarded as the main job of the child or youth. Edmund King (1967, 58) gives us an anecdote that illustrates the classic European attitude:

> An American mother who went to live in Paris was very proud of her two robust sons. A French neighbor was helpful and friendly, but one day she confided to the American mother that it was a pity her two sons looked so much like peasants. After a term in French schools, however, the American boys were so pale and tired from nightly homework that their mother was anxious. Just at this time the Frenchwoman congratulated her neighbor on the boys' development and stated that they now looked more like scholars.[12]

In contrast, the less positive attitude toward study effort in U.S. society manifests itself in many ways.[13] For example, in the current debate over lengthening the school year or day,[14] adults who object say they are concerned with the effects of too much study on their children's health, or they claim that heavier requirements would deprive young children of the wonderful experience of an American childhood. (Huck Finn has a lot to answer for here.) More serious study requirements also would restrict the time available to adolescents to participate in our youth culture. Finally, there is a widespread belief that too much study by children and teenagers will prevent them from becoming well-socialized, well-rounded American adults.

National Attitudes toward Study Effort: How Important Is It to Transmit the National Culture?

One interpretation of these ambiguous attitudes is that Americans do not place much emphasis on the transmission of culture and traditions to future generations. In most of the countries competing with us there is a wider acceptance of the view that learning the "higher culture" benefits both the individual and the nation.[15] It is perhaps more difficult here to explain American "exceptionalism" than the greater emphasis on learning a formal or traditional culture in many other societies.[16] In any event, a strong case can be made for including less positive attitudes about study effort in the United States as a fourth reason for the low esteem in which children hold study time.

In summary, there is a wide variety of explanations by psychologists and sociologists of student aversion to study effort. Youngsters come to see study as a challenge to their self-esteem; learning has become "decontextualized"; excessive exposure to television and popular music instills habits in young people which make it difficult to study; and the adult world doesn't really place much value on study effort or scholarly achievement. But whether or not we accept one or more of these various psychological and sociological explanations, we can, as economists, conclude that American children—at least those beyond the first few years of school—simply do not much like extra study time.

It may be possible that these attitudes will change. Any number of reformers have come forward with ideas for making school more enjoyable. Others would have society change the way children are socialized, teaching them to value intellectual effort for its own sake. For now we will take aversion to study as a given, to be dealt with as an obstacle to attempts to increase study effort.[17]

Other Activities Compete with Study Time

U.S. students don't just dislike study; they find that it interferes with other activities that they prefer, such as eating, sports, hobbies, listening to music, taking naps, and spending time with friends.[18] It is not surprising that much of their free time is spent on these activities.

Teenagers do not spend all their time outside school so pleasantly, however. Attitudes toward watching television are only marginally positive, ranking about halfway between doing homework and spending time with friends. Yet teenagers in the United States spend about as much time watching television as they do in school. Indeed, when it comes to hours spent in television viewing, the data indicate that our youth are world leaders.[19]

Moreover, while U.S. teenagers give hours spent at part-time jobs a much lower rating than television watching (it is at the same abysmal level as time devoted to homework or sitting in class), many adolescents spend much of their free time in these jobs, working afternoons or evenings or on the weekends.[20] This is in addition to the full-time jobs they may hold during their long summer holiday.

In the average working-class or middle-class neighborhood about one-half of the youths work during the school session, on average about fifteen or twenty hours per week.[21] Participation rates are somewhat lower in low-income neighborhoods, in which even full-time employment is scarce and often students cannot find part-time work, or among very affluent children (Greenberger and Steinberg 1986, 18–19; Sedlak and others 1986, 62). Overall, student part-time employment in the United States is far greater than in the nations that compete with us. In some of these countries employment is illegal for full-time students in state-supported schools. In most of the others it is kept to a very low level by family and social traditions.

Have the short schedules of our schools encouraged part-time work, or has the growth of part-time work encouraged schools to reduce their schedules and discouraged them from lengthening school hours? Students working fifteen to twenty hours a week at part-time jobs are clearly not in a position to treat their studies as a full-time occupation. We know, however, that students who devote to their educations the average number of hours a part-timer puts in at work do as well in school as those who do not work at all. The research indicates that students working longer hours (e.g., more than fifteen or twenty hours a week) achieve less in school, especially if this work begins in the earlier high school years (Greenberger and Steinberg 1986, 118).

The failure of work schedules of up to fifteen or twenty hours per week to damage school performance tells us a great deal about why our educational system is producing graduates whose skills do not match those of students in competing countries. Even if we posit an element of self-selection (i.e., that those teenagers who take part-time jobs tend to be those who think they have enough energy to handle their schoolwork and their duties on the job), this is still a telling indictment.[22]

It would be overstating the case, however, to argue that part-time job opportunities have *no* effect on student effort. In the hypothetical scenario in which school schedules are lengthened and homework assignments increased, part-time jobholders and their allies will resist. Students value their jobs, many parents support them, and school administrators often believe that student employment improves relationships with the community.[23] In that sense part-time work can be given some status as an independent factor in determining a student's degree of study effort. Nevertheless, it is likely that the low levels of effort required in the schools lead to increased part-time work, rather than the reverse.

We can analyze the other major activities engaged in by our youth when they are not studying, such as watching television, in the same way. Clearly, the minimal study effort put in by average high school students allows them to participate in passive leisure-time activities like sleeping, in addition to their part-time work and participation in more active youth culture activities like sports or dating. Of course, television influences the attitudes, expectations, and behaviors of youthful viewers, as well as others—seldom with a salutary effect on study effort. But other countries with widespread ownership of television sets manage to obtain high levels of study effort. Television sets, after all, can be turned off. It is difficult to put the major blame for our comparatively poor performance in schools on television, any more than on part-time work or the other activities that occupy the time of American adolescents.[24]

Chapter 3
Why Study?

The Rewards of Study and the Labor-Leisure Choice

If students lack interest in study and if, in addition, they find the youth culture more satisfactory, then the level of study effort must depend on extrinsic benefits—external rewards to the students who study and, possibly, penalties for those who do not.

An obvious parallel is the decision adults make about work, another activity that individuals would prefer not to take part in at all or, at least, for fewer hours per week, were it not for the external rewards. Adults, like students, have a myriad of activities they prefer to work, such as recreation or spending time with their children or spouse. The large literature on adult behavior in the labor market can be useful in analyzing the study effort of youths. We can then explain their study effort in terms of the extrinsic benefits that they believe it will bring, largely in adult life, such as higher income, better working conditions, and higher occupational status.[1]

Choosing Labor or Leisure

Economists assume that workers balance the utility (gain) from additional income against the disutility (pain) of the work effort required to obtain it. Workers desire both leisure, in the sense of time off from work, and consumption goods and services. Since the amount of goods and services consumed increases with wage income, the worker must decide how much leisure he or she will sacrifice in order to obtain more of these goods.

The theory predicts that if workers' income is increased, they will, ceteris paribus, choose more leisure as well as more consumption goods, so that labor supply decreases as income increases. But if the opportunity cost of their time (the amount of consumption the worker must give up to take an additional hour of leisure) is increased, then, ceteris paribus, their labor supply will increase. Workers who receive a substantial inheritance will probably reduce their work hours. On the other hand, workers offered overtime employment at double or triple pay will probably accept it.

When there is both an increase in the payoff to an additional hour of effort and a more general increase in income—as when income is raised by an across-the-board increase in the hourly wage rate—the effect on desired working hours is ambiguous. An across-the-board rise increases the opportunity cost of time in the same proportion that it raises income (if the worker has no property or other nonlabor income). Here the net effect on labor supply can only be determined empirically, by discovering which of the two effects has the greater impact on a given group of workers. If hours shrink when wages rise, we have the famous "backward-sloping supply curve of labor," which predicts a reduction in the supply of labor when wages increase.

We see this often in practice. For example, the long-term upward trend in real hourly wages in the United States has yielded a dramatic reduction in the hours of workers over the past century and a half. One can interpret this decline as evidence that the affluence yielded by higher wage rates offsets the effect of the higher opportunity cost of time, so that the demand for leisure has increased.

Does Affluence Explain the Decline in Study Effort?

Study effort and work effort are similar in that they both contribute to disutility, on the one hand, and to income, on the other. They can thus be treated as two aspects of a lifetime decision to supply effort. In this framework one can readily predict, for example, that a lifetime increase in the taste for leisure will decrease both study effort and later work effort. A lifetime increase in affluence will have a similar effect on both types of effort.

If this simple analogy could be applied without qualification, we could predict that the supply of study effort would rise or fall with the effort of adults. When that occurs the social cost of reducing hours is very great. The impact of lower work hours for adults is magnified, either by a reduction in the quality of the labor force or by an increase in educational costs. If the number of school years remains the same despite the reduction in study effort during those years, the proficiency of the work force will suffer. Alternatively, if proficiency is to be maintained, more years of schooling are required (with fewer years remaining for labor force participation), greatly increasing educational costs.

The total cost of reducing both student and adult hours would be about twice as high as that incurred if only adult hours were reduced (with student effort remaining constant).[2]

In fact, however, adult and student hours only move together in the very long run.[3] In the 1960s and 1970s, when most observers believe that study effort suffered, the working hours of adult males remained stable, large numbers of adult women entered the labor force, and real hourly wages, which had been rising rapidly, began to stagnate.

Such anomalies suggest that a more complex analysis than the backward-sloping-supply-curve-of-labor theory outlined above is needed to explain the low level of study effort.[4] Since other influences have also been at work, we cannot link lackadaisical student behavior to our affluence in any simple way, such as predicting the reaction of an individual worker to a change in his or her wage. Fortunately, much of the interesting research on the supply of labor to the market in the past thirty years has also gone beyond the simple model. Now that two-earner families have become the norm, the assumption that labor supply decisions are made by independent individuals has been dropped, and economists treat them as part of family decision making. Similarly, as retirement has become a more important labor supply issue, there has been a growing interest in how individuals react to rewards and incentives that will only be available in the distant future—for example, to predict how much effect a change in pension policy will have on the age of employee retirement. Finally, nowadays most of us do not face a constant return to our effort but, instead, are confronted by progressive income taxes or limits on our earnings if we wish to continue to receive Social Security pensions or government transfers such as food stamps. Hence, analyzing situations in which the marginal return to effort is not the same as the average return is important. (E.g., we want empirical evidence to back up the commonsense view that, when the marginal return is less than the average return, effort is likely to suffer.)

These several innovations in economic analysis are most useful in studying the determination of student effort. More specifically, three types of departures from the standard model can be employed. First, since students do not make decisions on study effort independently but are, instead, influenced by their parents, a family analysis is appropriate. Second, while adults get monetary rewards at the end of each pay period, the financial payoff to study effort is distant and somewhat uncertain, so that an analysis that considers the whole life cycle is needed. Third, the link between returns and study effort is weak. The labor market determines the reward to study; schools do not. (In contrast, the efforts of adult workers are directly rewarded by their employers.) Because the flow of information between school and employer in the United States is badly flawed, adolescents who do study hard in school often do not get rewarded proportionately later.

Changes in Family Decision Making

Clearly, the decision making of a child or adolescent is different from that of an adult, since parents exercise some control over, or at least influence, study effort. In the first place, parents must support full-time students financially. Children may have to leave school at the legal age of sixteen without family support; with it students may pursue their studies until they are well into their twenties. In the second place, parents can influence the amount of study their children do while in school; they can, for example, guide children to an appropriate curriculum and insist on some rules for homework and other study time. At the same time students can impose their own limits on parental control, using a variety of strategies to resist their demands.

Economists have generally modeled family decision making in the context of the labor and leisure allocations of husbands and wives, rather than parents and children.[5] In some models spouses cooperate fully: they consider the productivity of each partner in the home and in the market as well as the preferences each has for different types of activities and agree on an outcome that maximizes family welfare. More recent models seek to be more realistic by taking into account family conflicts and their resolution (Kooreman and Kapteyn 1990; McElroy 1990).

These spousal models can be applied to the parent-child relationship.[6] The conflict resolution approach is definitely needed here. While one expects a measure of agreement between parents and children on study time (most youngsters would probably concede that some effort is desirable), there is less likelihood of consensus on a level of study. Conflicts over study effort may be due to objective or subjective differences. Objective differences can arise when a parent is less than altruistic and makes decisions on the basis of his or her own utility, rather than that of his or her child. For example, a mother may feel that, if her son studies hard, he will eventually become a doctor, gaining status for the family and, perhaps, taking care of her in her old age. As a result, the mother may put a much lower value on the leisure of her teenager than would be the case if she gave the teenager's utility a weight equal to her own.

Even if parents are completely altruistic and give full weight to the happiness of their children, more subjective differences can yield different preferred allocations concerning homework time. Parents may have greater experience, knowledge, and maturity, but they may also forget what it is like to be a child. More generally, we will expect that the notoriously high discount youths put on the future will lead them to prefer a lower level of study effort than their parents would wish. In brief, whether differences occur because of selfish disputes or because of a different perspective on what is best for the child, parent-child conflict is in most cases inevitable and will undoubtedly influence outcomes.

The economic literature on family conflict has to be modified to apply to the parent-child relationship, since parents have a moral and legal power over their children which is not available between spouses. Indeed, in some ways the parent-child relationship is more like that between employers and employees. Employers give instructions to employees, who may or may not execute them.[7] To determine whether orders are being obeyed, employers can monitor workers in a variety of ways, assigning supervisors to observe employees or otherwise carefully measuring the quality and quantity of their work. To be effective, monitoring must be accompanied by sanctions and rewards—dismissal for "shirking" and, for good performance, retention, a pay raise, and, possibly, a promotion. Because monitoring and surveillance are expensive, and because severe penalties for shirking can hurt employee morale and increase the turnover rate, employers typically learn to live with a certain amount of shirking.

Similarly, parents can hope to enhance their influence on their children's behavior, if they are willing to invest their own time and money. They can spend time observing their children, rewarding those who do their homework and penalizing those who do not. If they are affluent, they can hire and train a nanny to do much the same thing. In practice many parents, like employers, will decide that they have to learn to live with a certain amount of shirking.

Of course, the use of time and money are only two aspects of the effort parents make to obtain compliance by their children. With greater or less success they try to induce children to internalize their own norms, thus minimizing the need for monitoring their behavior or providing sanctions.[8] Nevertheless, time and, in some instances, money are important inputs.

These conflicts between parents and children are hardly new. The approach used to analyze disputes between parents and children over the issue of homework in 1944 can be used in 1994. Then, as now, parents generally wanted their children to do more studying than the children wanted to do or could be induced to do without unusual pressure.[9] It is likely, though, that the problem has worsened over the past several decades. If the opportunity cost of parents' time increases, so that they spend less time monitoring their children, shirking—for example, children devoting less time to homework than parents would like—will increase.[10] More shirking will be tolerated, too, if society gives less support to parents who strictly control their children.

In the period when effort devoted to homework appears to have declined in the United States, the number of two-parent, one-wage-earner families sharply declined. The increased proportion of mothers of school-age children who work full-time and the smaller proportion who have a husband living with them reduced the time available for parental monitoring. At the same time parental authority was being challenged, and societal attitudes and legal decisions undermined the ability of schools to stand in loco parentis to enforce discipline codes. These economic and social changes very likely moved the actual study level away from that preferred by parents and closer to the lower level preferred by students (quite apart from any decline in the levels of study effort preferred either by students or parents).

Distant and Uncertain Rewards as Weak Incentives

As previously noted, adult work is rewarded fairly promptly, at the end of the week or month,[11] while students begin to receive their financial reward a decade or so later and continue to receive it in installments over a working life of forty or more years.[12] Partly because they have to wait so long to reap these benefits, they cannot be certain about how much their effort will pay off.

Economic theory and empirical evidence predict that rewards that are distant and uncertain will be heavily discounted, by adults as well as by children (Ghez and Becker 1975; Owen 1986). Since the return to study effort is uncertain as well as deferred, it is not surprising that students discount it. This weakens their incentive to study. Moreover, because students tend to discount the future at a higher rate than adults, a long delay in receiving uncertain rewards exacerbates the conflict between parents and children over the issue of study time.[13]

The last generation has seen a sharp increase in the number of years spent in school, so that the average student today must wait longer before he or she can begin to earn a full-time wage than those in earlier times. Even after they have finished school high school graduates must wait longer to get a well-paying job; today many employers have become reluctant to hire recent graduates. (This argument is explored further in chap. 5.)

Grades and School Prizes as Motivators

While adult workers sell their labor directly to firms and obtain their rewards from them, students supply their labor to schools and must look to another institution, the firm, for any financial rewards. This distinction has important consequences.

Neither the level of effort required by schools nor the school's curriculum need correspond to the preferences of children or their parents. When adults sell their labor to a competitive, profit-maximizing firm, economic theory predicts that conditions of employment, including the number of hours of work, will tend to move toward the level preferred by the average employee (always taking into account the costs that the employer incurs in providing these conditions). Employers want to minimize their labor costs by hiring workers at the lowest hourly wage (other things being equal). If they can lower wages or other costs by changing a work schedule to one that is preferred by the workers, they will do so.[14] The theory predicts that, if workers are asked whether they would like to change their hours of work with a proportionate change in their weekly wages or maintain their schedules, the largest number would choose to retain their present schedule: there would not be a majority of employees in favor of either more or fewer hours of work. Susan Shank (1986) cites a recent national study that found just this result in the United States.

Schools operate on different principles. True, one could design a theoretical model of schools that, like a competitive labor market, offered considerable choice. Students, acting under the guidance of their parents, could freely choose the level of effort, in effect deciding how much learning they would accomplish each year (and, hence, how much of an increase in future earning power they would be able to achieve) at a given sacrifice of leisure. This would more closely approximate the typical employer-employee relationship.[15]

The reality, however, is quite different. In the United States the dominant public school system is a set of overlapping governmental bureaucracies, each with its own goals. While individual families do have some influence on the system, and parents and children as a group can affect it, to some extent, through the political process, many others, including outsiders representing larger or smaller constituencies and career bureaucrats employed by the school system, endeavor to control the schools.[16] As a result, school policies may only weakly correspond to the wishes of individual parents and their children.

Similarly, the curriculum itself is designed with an eye to social and political interests, not just the individual's future economic success in the labor market or other individual goals. Partly for this reason, the rewards distributed by the school system for success in meeting its requirements, such as good grades and honors, need not correspond well with the kinds of learning which will be valued in the labor market or that will serve other interests of the family. Students are thus working for tokens, or credentials, which may or may not have a cash value in the labor market in the future, as well as learning skills that have a more obvious relationship with future employment. The lack of a tangible reward further weakens student incentives (see chap. 6).

Perhaps the most negative effect of the separation of schools and employment on incentives to study is that information about the work and accomplishments of a student must be conveyed to another institution, the firm, if students are to receive full credit for their work. In later chapters I describe in some detail the failure of our system to transmit and process this information efficiently, a major factor in the low level of study effort in the United States.

Explaining Increases in Student Employment

The growth of student part-time work is not simply a result of the willingness of young people to supply their labor; it also reflects an increased market demand for them. Growth has not been steady and linear: the nature and purpose of student part-time jobs has changed over the years. In the nineteenth and even the early twentieth centuries children lived largely in rural areas, where they were usefully employed, typically on the family farm, doing farm chores after school, on weekends, and over the relatively long summer holiday. Our unusually short school schedules reflect century-old accommodations to the needs of an agrarian life-style.

As the population became more urbanized in the earlier years of this century, there was less demand for student labor. Still, some students were able to work in a family business, while others found part-time employment outside the home, working at such jobs as selling newspapers or making deliveries for stores. Student part-time employment grew rapidly in the years following the end of World War II, in part because there was an increased employer demand for it in the retail trade and personal services sectors.[17] These sectors have always afforded opportunities to part-timers, and their rapid growth has itself provided new openings. In addition, the proportion of part-timers in these sectors grew. Part-timers have played a useful role in closing the scheduling gaps caused by reductions in the working times of full-time employees, on the one hand, and longer hours of operation in many outlets, on the other (Owen 1979, 1986). Retail and service outlets in or near residential areas are especially attractive to local students seeking work after school.

Everyday evidence of the importance of the demand for part-time workers in determining employment rates is its geographical distribution. Rates are typically much lower in the inner city—where many youngsters are eager for work but where there are few part-time opportunities—than in the suburbs, where employers are seeking part-time workers.[18]

The increased demand for student part-time employment has facilitated its growth; without this rising demand, the effect of an increased number of students seeking jobs would have been a glut, with the likelihood of greater unemployment and reduced wages (Owen 1986).

Modern part-time employment differs in a number of ways from earlier times. First, student workers tend to be older, largely because Americans stay in school longer than they used to but also because child labor laws restrict the employment of young children. Student employees today are typically adolescents, fourteen years of age or older. In the past most adolescents either participated in the labor force full-time or stayed home helping with housework.

Second, there has been a change in the class composition of student part-timers. In the early years of this century those who were in high school were generally from relatively more affluent homes, did not need to work, and, in fact, usually stayed out of the labor force. By the 1940s high school enrollment had greatly expanded, and many of the working-class children who now attended school held part-time jobs. High school students from the better-off families typically did not work (Hollingshead 1949). Today part-time jobs are held by youths from comparatively affluent families as well as by those less well-off; children from the poorest neighborhoods often cannot find work.

Third, the opportunities for part-time work available today are less likely to lead to high-status jobs. Part-time jobs are typically not on a family farm or in a family business, nor are they often located in factories or offices that offer promising careers. Instead, they tend to be "dead-end," entry-level jobs in the retail trade or service sector, usually in the suburban areas where the teenagers live. These new jobs typically require little cognitive achievement, offer few job training opportunities, entail work under close (often authoritarian) supervision, and are age-segregated, with limited opportunities for student part-timers to interact with adult coworkers (Greenberger and Steinberg 1986, 151–55).

The present pattern is also different in that most student part-time workers do not give a significant portion of their earnings to their families (ibid.). In earlier times, when a child worked on the family farm or in the family business, parents received the fruits of the child's labor and decided how to distribute them. If youngsters did earn income outside the home, they were typically asked to contribute part or all of their earnings to the family. In contrast, student earners today keep most or all of their pay and use it to sustain their involvement in an expensive youth culture. Automobiles, clothes, stereo equipment, CDs and tapes, and meals away from home absorb most of their earnings (Bachman, Johnston, and O'Malley 1984, 94; Greenberger and Steinberg 1986, 30–37). Taken together, these factors have transformed the student part-time labor market into its modern form—one in which older students, of average economic status, work in jobs that have little long-term payoff and use most of their earnings for what would not very long ago have been called luxuries.

Why Do Students Take Part-Time Jobs?

If the greater demand for part-time workers has contributed to the growth of student employment, the low level of study effort required by schools or demanded by parents has facilitated it: requirements at, say, the Japanese level would eliminate the student part-time job market in its present form. These findings explain why students can find part-time jobs and stay in them without failing in school, but they do not explain why students take jobs in the first place. We are left with an apparent paradox: If young people study less in order to have more leisure, why do they trade so much of their time for part-time jobs? Youths holding down part-time jobs of fifteen or twenty hours a week have even less leisure time than young people in countries whose study requirements are more rigorous than ours. A shift from study effort to part-time work cannot be regarded as a shift from a less to a more pleasant activity, since, as noted in chapter 2, the average student does not enjoy his or her job.

Should we treat student part-time work as a leisure-time activity? Or should we regard both part-time work for pay and study effort as components of the "labor supply" of adolescents? In work, as in study, a youth sacrifices leisure time to obtain economic and other rewards. If this argument were accepted without qualification, one could then question the need for separate analyses of the two activities.

In fact, there are important distinctions between these two forms of labor supply. They respond to different stimuli. Student part-time work has risen rapidly in the past several decades, while study effort is said to have declined, in a period of very little growth in the real hourly wage rate or in general economic well-being. The recent spurt in part-time working by students cannot readily be attributed either to a higher price of time or to increased affluence, two traditional explanations of labor supply changes.

A better understanding of why more and more students are choosing to work in part-time jobs can be derived from Gary Becker's theory of "leisure activities" (1965). Becker argues that individuals do not seek leisure time or consumer goods and services as such but, instead, pursue pleasant activities that require time as well as goods and services. Free time and consumer goods and services are valued only insofar as they contribute to these activities. Leisure, or recreational, activities—typically defined as activities with a high time-to-goods ratio—are one class of pleasant activities. Applying Becker's theory to student part-time work, we start by observing that teenagers today believe that their leisure activities require, or at least benefit from, a variety of material inputs, such as special clothing, stereo equipment, a car, a large collection of CDs and tapes, food and drink, and outlays on expensive dates. They combine these goods and services with leisure time to produce pleasant activities, just as their parents combine goods and time to provide themselves with satisfying recreational activities (Becker 1965; Owen 1969). Part-time jobs enable young people to purchase the inputs they need for a high level of Beckerian leisure activities; in a word, they yield the material basis of our famous youth culture.

If students contributed their earnings to the total family budget, and if a portion of this budget was routinely allocated to youth culture purchases, regardless of whether the youth was employed, a very different type of analysis would be needed. But we know from survey data that most students keep what they earn and that parents are generally unwilling to subsidize youth culture purchases—at least not to the extent that they are willing to provide a nutritious diet, warm clothing, and decent housing.[19]

This somewhat incongruous outcome can be interpreted as a classic application of family conflict theory. In a parallel case the theory explains why wives would sometimes enter the labor market even when, in earlier times, the value of their time in the market was less than the value of their time at home. When earning money outside the home gives the employed family member more power in determining the outcome of family decisions, such as how the family budget will be allocated, a wife may experience an increase in her utility by working, whether or not the family as a whole is better off. Similarly, an important motive for student employment is to obtain a degree of direct control over a portion of the family income. It is, in essence, a way of resolving conflicts between parents and teenagers over how family income shall be spent, assuming, of course, that there is prior agreement on a rule about this part-time work and how the money will be spent—for example, if adolescents seek and find part-time employment, they may use their earnings as they like.

Sacrificing the Future

If we accept the treatment of part-time work as an input in leisure activities, part-time work yields more, not less, leisure activity for youths. It does, however, have less favorable consequences for the enjoyment of activities over the life cycle, since enjoying a high level of leisure activities as an adolescent imposes future costs (Ghez and Becker 1975; Owen 1986). It takes time away from study (the time spent in part-time employment to earn money for leisure activities plus the leisure time itself), and this reduction in study effort will reduce future income and, thus, the quality of leisure and other consumption activities that the youth can look forward to as an adult.[20]

Keep in mind that teenagers are maximizing their lifetime utility *as they see it*. If they discount the future heavily, they will want to provide themselves with enjoyable leisure activities now, at the expense of high-quality activities as adults. The positive result is that the level of leisure activity enjoyed by American youths today is far higher than it was fifty or one hundred years ago, when youngsters had less free time and, when they did take time out, engaged in less expensive leisure-time activities. A decline in extracurricular activities in our high schools has been observed as part-time jobs become more common. These extra-curricular activities, which are usually free, or nearly so, to the student, often take place in the late afternoon, when many students are at their part-time jobs.

The substitution of part-time employment for study effort need not be interpreted as an increased preference either for work or for leisure. There are several plausible supply-side explanations for it, including:

- A high, and possibly rising, rate of preference for present consumption over saving for the future. Some argue that U.S. society is experiencing a higher rate of time preference and point to lower savings rates and higher debt levels as evidence. Substituting participation in the youth culture for study effort further supports this view.

- A weakening of family ties between spouses and between generations. Young people are imitating their parents in demanding and getting some control over how they spend their time. This increased autonomy permits adolescents to substitute their own high rate of time preference for that of their parents.

- Less objective incentive to study while in school.

II INCENTIVES TO STUDY

Chapter 4

Does Studying Pay? Returns to Those Staying in School

A vast majority of students think that there is no need to concentrate on the acquisition of knowledge in high school, and as a result, most have become progressively disengaged from the academic experience. For many students the meaning of high school and the alternative options available for investing energy and time are such that there is little incentive to be heavily involved in academic learning.

Sedlak and others 1986

The expectation that spending time in school will yield higher earnings in later life can offer an important incentive for students. Economists have developed several theories to explain the relationship between earnings and education.

Predictions from Human Capital Theory

The classic, or human capital, view, as expressed by Gary Becker (1975), is that education increases the productivity of young people by teaching them marketable skills and that this productivity is later rewarded when the graduate enters the labor market. The gain in the individual's productivity takes two forms, improvements in cognitive achievement and in socialization. Cognitive achievement includes such general skills as reading, writing, and mathematics. It can also include occupation-specific skills, such as typing, reading a blueprint, or operating a lathe. Socialization includes acquiring a wide variety of social skills, such as learning to work with others, to take orders from supervisors (or to give them to those who report to you), and to behave responsibly on the job—not to steal, fight, or take drugs, to show up for work on time and do a reasonable amount of work while there, and to care about the quality of output. It also includes such complex skills as those needed to make a presentation to a client or to present a creative suggestion to an employer. As the diversity of these examples makes clear, different jobs require different types of socialization as well as different types of cognitive achievement.[1]

This human capital theory predicates a direct relationship between work in school and later earnings. In the simplest version of the theory the problem of conveying information from schools to employers either doesn't exist or is irrelevant: young employees know which firm will find them most useful, and potential employers will pay them in accordance with their contributions. A more realistic version admits some frictional adjustments—delays in matching employers and employees, for example, or in discovering the merits of workers and paying them accordingly. The theory, though, argues that employers and employees will then be appropriately matched in a competitive labor market and that the various skills and attributes of graduates will, on average, be appropriately rewarded as a result.

The Screening Theory of Returns to Schooling

According to the screening theory, schools generate and transmit appropriate information, or "signals," about job applicants to employers.[2] The educational process lasts from ten to sixteen or more years and generates a large amount of data about individual students: grade point average (GPA); choice of a solid curriculum versus nonchallenging, or "Mickey Mouse," courses; scores on tests such as the SAT and American College Testing exam (ACT); participation in extracurricular activities; letters of recommendation; various disciplinary records; and the diploma itself.

Some economists see the production of information about individual students as the principal, if not the sole, function of education. As Kenneth Wolpin (1977, 950) explains, "In the most extreme form of the screening hypothesis, schooling serves only to identify those individuals who are more productive . . . the proposition being that an individual's productivity is unaffected by the formal schooling process."

Michael Sedlak, a noneconomist and a perspicacious observer of our school system, presents one of the more extreme versions of the theory. He argues that, in the nineteenth century, our high school system changed from being a producer of skills to being a useful screen. At one time the high school curriculum helped to prepare a relatively small student body for occupations that required an academic education or for further study. Yet, as enrollment rose sharply in the first half of this century, the proportion of graduates taking clerical, sales, or similar white-collar jobs increased. The academic subjects studied in high school were of little direct use in these occupations. Nevertheless, according to Sedlak, a high school diploma continued to serve as a useful screen for white-collar employment, since only the more able and industrious students finished high school.[3]

A more realistic version of this theory does not completely reject the human capital notion but holds that information as well as improved skills and performance are produced by the educational system. Screening theory implies that the value of a degree to the student is reduced unless schools provide accurate information about individual achievement. In deciding how much to pay a new hire, the employers must consider how productive the applicant will be on the job. The absence of accurate information about applicants makes it difficult to predict how satisfactory they will be on the job and, hence, what would be an appropriate wage offer. For example, in the absence of good information, if all graduates from one of the local high schools are given the same credit for educational attainment, and paid at roughly the same rate, the more able will be underpaid and the low achievers overpaid.

The screening theorists also make a less obvious point: that the average wage paid to these graduates will be below that paid if employers actually knew their achievements, and hence their expected productivity. Because jobs typically require special skills or aptitudes, employers need to select those employees likely to be trainable for the positions available. In the absence of good information, round pegs will inevitably be placed in square holes: an employee with an aptitude for spatial relations, for example, will be assigned to a task requiring strong verbal skills. Such a mismatch is costly to employers. The screening theory predicts that, when accurate information about the individual is important, applicants for whom this information is lacking will either not be hired or, if hired, will on average be paid less.

The preference of employers for certainty over risk when making a hiring decision provides a second reason for underpaying employees in the absence of good information. Risk aversion can be an important motive, even when there is no danger of misassigning an employee. Consider, for example, a typing job for which someone who types twice as fast as another is simply worth twice as much to the employer. Risk-averse employers will pay less when they are uncertain about the applicant's speed (Wolpin 1977). If the employer believes, for example, that there is a one-third chance that an applicant's typing speed is 80 words per minute, a one-third chance that it is 50 words per minute, and a one-third chance that it is 110 words per minute, then the expected value of the applicant's typing speed is 80 words per minute. But if the employer doesn't want to risk hiring a slow typist (as might be the case if only one person is being hired), the pay offer will be less than if it were certain that the applicant can type 80 words per minute.

A more moderate version of the screening theory, in which schools both increase the student's productivity and generate useful information, also predicts a *delayed* return to schooling achievements when schools provide less than perfect measures of student achievement. Since an appropriate assignment and pay scale is then unlikely, graduates can expect to work in jobs for which the variance in skills among employees does not disrupt the production process. If the employees' performance on these jobs yields reliable information about their potential, employers can later assign them to more suitable jobs and pay them accordingly. Even if employers do not choose to reassign new hires within the organization, successful employees can often take their experience and résumés to a new employer who offers a more satisfactory job. For most, reassignment or relocation means improvement. It is true that certain employees find that their earnings have declined to correct for an original overestimation of their abilities. But if the misclassification and risk aversion arguments are correct, and the average wage paid in the absence of good information is lower than if employers knew more about those they are considering for jobs, then this *average* wage will rise as better information is acquired in the first years of employment experience.

Finally, screening theory is helpful in forecasting the result when schools generate information that is irrelevant or actually misleading to employers making hiring decisions. In practice employers often find that school-based information about applicants is poorly designed. A school may see its role not as improving the earnings prospects of graduates but, rather, as developing in them an appreciation of the "higher culture" or good citizenship qualities, and training and evaluating students accordingly.[4] In that case a high ranking could mean that a student has a good command of the Latin classics or is currently an avid reader of the *New York Times*, rather than reflecting skills or work habits that would interest employers. Another school might develop a pattern of behavior in its students which would be useful to employers but is not likely to be maintained in real-life employment situations. For example, some private boarding schools impose rigid behavior codes, but employers do not know for certain whether the schools' graduates will maintain these habits when they are in a less structured environment. On the other hand, while many other schools tolerate poor behavior by students, such as tardiness or failure to do homework, an employer considering one of these schools' graduates can expect that at least some of them will "shape up" when put in a demanding, real-life employment situation. Finally, schools may deliberately generate misleading signals about their graduates to further their own institutional goals (these practices are discussed at length in chap. 6).

The theory predicts that, while, in the short run, employers may accept credentials from unreliable schools as valid, they will eventually learn to discount them. Some employers will make an effort to interpret confusing or misleading transcripts in terms of their own needs; many will simply avoid hiring graduates from schools that provide poor information or, on average, poor graduates; still others will ignore recent graduates altogether in favor of people who have proven themselves over several years of work experience.

Does Study Effort Actually Pay Off?
The Return to Staying in School Is High and Rising

There is good evidence that staying in school yields a substantial economic gain to students.[5] It has been, and continues to be, a good investment,[6] even in a dynamic economy in which both the occupational distribution of the labor force and the educational attainment of workers have changed radically. The occupational opportunities available at different levels of schooling also have changed sharply; in general, more education is now required for the same occupation. Despite these changes, additional schooling continues to yield the individual greater income and status.

As the economy has developed, the nature of the return from each level of schooling has changed. A degree that was once the mark of membership in an elite group has become commonplace. At the same time the lack of a degree has become a stigma; its value remains high (Markey 1988; Mathios 1989). A good example is the high school diploma. At one time no additional education was needed to rise to the ranks of upper management in a typical firm. Later, high school graduates were likely to get white-collar employment. Moreover, if they were both industrious and intelligent—and fortunate in their choice of organization—they still had considerable upward mobility, even if a position in top management was unlikely.

As education levels continued to increase in the 1960s and 1970s, however, the majority of students got high school diplomas, and more and more of the better-paying factory jobs required them.[7] In the 1990s most new high school graduates will go into service jobs, lower-level factory work, and the like (see the discussion in chap. 5). Management specialists tell us that in a very few years the better-paying entry-level jobs in our automated factories will demand an associate's degree, requiring two years of postsecondary education. Yet, in spite of the continued decline in the status of high school graduates, the return to a high school diploma in the United States remains at a satisfactory level. It holds its value because a minority of young people lack it and are relegated to ever lower positions in the economy.

The vast increase in the supply of people with degrees and diplomas has been accompanied by vast changes in the occupational structure and the educational demands of most employers. The net result has been a return on years of schooling which has, on average, been fairly good.

How Much Studying Do U.S. Schools Require?

The return to study effort is more ambiguous. A good return to staying in school need not translate into a strong incentive to study while there; most students do not see a need for long hours of study in order to remain in school. In fact, in most districts, the average student need invest relatively little effort to complete the entire K–12 sequence. Students are sometimes passed to the next grade regardless of their academic performance. Where this "social pass" system is not in place, students can often find easy courses and teachers, enabling them to obtain at least a minimal grade and thus be able to move to the next year.

According to some historians, the amount of study effort needed to finish high school has gradually declined, as secondary education has been extended to ever larger groups of students. Others reject this assessment, pointing to even poorer performance by students in the period before World War II (Bishop 1989c; Murray and Herrnstein 1992).

Over the past several years there has been some tightening of standards. The very worst abuses have been curtailed or eliminated by mandating better course syllabi in the weakest schools using National Assessment of Educational Progress results to highlight shortcomings, for example, and introducing minimum achievement requirements for graduation.[8] But the majority of students still find it quite easy to finish the first twelve years of school.

Calculating the effects of student effort during elementary and high school on college attendance is more complex. If a youngster wants to attend one of the nation's most prestigious colleges or to obtain a college scholarship, high grades in school and, especially, high scores on general tests of learning and scholastic aptitude, such as the SAT and ACT exams, are mandatory (McPartland and others 1986). Likewise, students who want to go on in school but are for some reason disadvantaged—having limited intellectual abilities, coming from poor family backgrounds, or attending schools that are substantially below national standards—typically must work hard to meet the standards of even the least demanding postsecondary institutions. In practice many of them are discouraged from going further, and often they do not pursue their educations further.

However, average students in the United States who settle for a college that is not in the elite group, well aware that successful business or professional careers have been launched by graduates from quite ordinary institutions, feel little pressure to work hard.

As the college system has expanded, the number of institutions accepting applicants with fairly modest credentials has also grown. The great expansion in the supply of places in the higher education system in the past forty years, partly to accommodate the baby boom generation, has now outpaced student demand, the baby boomers now having been replaced by those of the so-called baby bust. Schools have been scrambling to fill their classrooms. Chester Finn (1991, 113) calculates that only fifty U.S. "colleges and universities . . . accept fewer than half of their applicants out of some 3,400 degree offering campuses and an additional 8,500 'noncollege' providers of postsecondary education. Perhaps 200 more institutions are somewhat selective, accepting fifty to ninety percent of those who apply."

The best evidence of how easy it is to pursue some form of postsecondary education in the United States is that almost half of all high school graduates do so, despite what we know to be a very low average level of study effort.

Chapter 5

The Return to Those Who Leave School

Many employers require a high school diploma for all new hires, yet very few believe that the diploma indicates educational achievement. More than 90% view the [high school] diploma as a sign of the applicant's reliability and staying power, proof only that they did not drop out. . . . [T]he non–college bound know that their performance in high school is likely to have little or no bearing on the type of employment they manage to find.

Commission on the Skills of the American Workforce 1990

Taking solid courses, attending classes regularly, and doing homework do yield academic achievement. The earnings of recent high school graduates and dropouts, however, do not strongly reflect these accomplishments.[1]

John Bishop (1990) has recently done pioneering work on the relationship between achievement and earnings. In a study of the earnings of a panel of Americans in their early and middle twenties, Bishop finds that ability has little effect:[2] *"High level academic competencies do not have positive effects on wage rates and earnings."* In fact, he points out, "the Mathematics Reasoning, Verbal and Science composites all have negative effects on wage rates and earning and often positive effects on unemployment. Speed in Arithmetic Computation has substantial positive effects on labor market success of young men. This competency, however, is a lower-order skill that is not (and should not be) a focus of high school mathematics."

Bishop is more positive about less traditional subjects. For young men "technical subtests measuring Electronics Knowledge and Mechanical, Auto and Shop Information have large and significant positive effects on wage rates and earnings and negative effects on unemployment" (108).[3] Courses in typing and other secretarial skills have long been used by young women to obtain employment upon graduation from high school. For older workers, however, academic achievement seems to have a better payoff. Bishop's study of male heads of households 25 to 64 years of age showed a significant correlation between a measure of "general intellectual achievement" and earnings. An increase of 11 to 19 percent in earnings was associated with a one standard deviation increase in this measure of achievement (Bishop 1989c, 181).[4]

Taken together, these recent studies imply that academic achievements have very little impact in the years right after high school graduation, although they probably increase earnings in later life. Moreover, measures of the effect of achievement on earnings may actually overestimate the impact of study effort. People who leave school with high levels of academic accomplishment tend to have qualities that will stand them in good stead later in life. Academic accomplishment is correlated with the intelligence quotient of youngsters and with the socioeconomic status of their families as well as with their willingness to work. It is not surprising, then, that those who do well in high school accomplish more than others, say, twenty or thirty years after graduation. The attributes that helped the student to do well in school will likely help the employee to learn on-the-job skills and to deal intelligently with a variety of work situations. To interpret the correlation between achievement and later earnings as a cause-and-effect relationship between study effort and earnings would overstate the case (Gottfredson 1984).[5] Clearly, much more research is needed on this issue.

Nevertheless, in the absence of better data, we will assume that study effort may pay off in later life but does not pay off right away. It fits the picture of the relationship between school and work drawn by investigators using nonstatistical techniques. The question is: Why is this so?

The most obvious explanation is that employers are often ignorant of applicants' academic accomplishments. Schools collect a great deal of information about their students. Data on deportment and attendance, together with course information, could tell employers a great deal. Of course, much of what is learned in school is not directly relevant to an employment situation, and much of the information schools pass on to employers is confusing or even deliberately misleading. As a result, according to the Commission on the Skills of the American Workforce (1990, 45), employers "realized long ago that it is possible to graduate from high school in this country and still be functionally illiterate."

Most employers use very little of the information that they do get. Some show little interest in educational credentials; others simply want to know whether the applicant has a degree or diploma; still others want details about the school's curriculum or the student's GPA. Some employers will request information directly from the school, while others will accept the applicant's own word. The majority, however, make little use of the high school record. A national study of major employers found that the "vast majority do not even ask to see a transcript" (ibid., 45). A recent national study of small and medium-sized employers (Bishop 1989a) found that only 14 percent obtained transcripts before selecting a high school graduate. One reason why they do not request records is that schools often do not make them available in time to make an employment decision. To obtain information more quickly, an employer can ask the applicant directly to describe his or her high school performance. Most do not. Only 15 percent asked graduates to report their grades. According to John Bishop (1989a, 32), "The absence of questions about grades from most job applications reflects the low reliability of self-reported data [and] the difficulties of verifying it."[6]

Achievement and aptitude tests provide an alternative for assessment. Industrial psychologists have found that "scores on tests measuring competence in reading, mathematics, science and problem solving are strongly related to productivity in almost all the civilian jobs studied" (ibid., 31). But the employer survey cited above found only 3 percent using them.[7] As a result, "American employers generally lack objective information on applicant accomplishments, skills and productivity."

Fear of violating civil rights laws discourages employers from using high school records or their own tests. Differences between the cognitive achievement levels of blacks and whites with the same number of years of schooling mean that tests measuring achievement in areas such as reading, writing, and mathematics often favor whites. Under present law employers must demonstrate that any test that has such "disparate impact" is relevant or necessary for a job. In practice it is very difficult to predict how the Equal Employment Opportunity Commission (EEOC) or the courts will interpret these rules in particular instances. As a result, while "employers are enthusiastic about [educational] reform . . . when you ask them individually to give greater weight to academic achievement in their own hiring, they say that we need to talk to [our] lawyer first" (Bishop 1991, 514). Some employers do not even ask to see transcripts, reasoning that if they do not know a minority student's grades, IQ, or disciplinary record, they cannot be accused of using this material to discriminate.

It is not surprising that the most important determinant of whether recent high school graduates are hired and the wages they are offered is performance during the employment interview (McPartland and others 1986; Crain 1984).

The screening theory implies that, unless good information is communicated to employers, they will not hire recent graduates for positions that require a satisfactory level of academic achievement. Survey data indicate that employers who do hire recent high school graduates or dropouts typically offer them jobs requiring only a minimal amount of traditional academic attainment. These include some of the worst jobs available, often poorly paid positions in the service sector which require little skill.[8] A study by Richard Miguel and Robert Faulk (1984, 17) of youths who had been out of high school one year found that 43 percent were in fast food, grocery, and retail sales work, 25 percent in other largely service jobs, and 32 percent in offices and factories.

In these cases employers often do not bother to sort students out because most high school graduates function well enough in low-skill jobs. Using years of schooling as a screen (along with an interview, including some perfunctory questions about school performance), they get a reasonable mix of cognitive skills "caught up in the net" of new employees, to be sorted out later.

Employers often complain about young hires' lack of noncognitive skills, reflected in such things as poor attendance records, difficulties working and communicating with others and in following instructions, and negative attitudes toward learning new job skills. A study by J. P. Lisack and Kevin Shell (1988, 3) of unskilled, entry-level jobs found that hindrances to hiring or retention included, in order of importance: attendance problems; poor work record and unreliability on the job; unwillingness or inability to learn; drug or alcohol problems; and disciplinary problems and inability to get along with others. Low academic and job skill levels were only in sixth place. As a result, when these employers select candidates they give more weight to their estimate of how well applicants are socialized than to their academic attainments. For example, the Commission on the Skills of the American Workforce (1990, 24) found that, when considering applicants without a college education, "the primary concern of more than 80 percent of employers is finding workers with a good work ethic and appropriate social behavior." Yet schools generally do not pass on to these employers the information that might be useful to them—the disciplinary records of students.

Even when work in school does contribute to the on-the-job productivity of young people, it may not increase their wages in the short run. Most employers don't vary wages among employees at a given job in proportion to individual productivity differences—not even when they actually observe these differences and even when the differences are important (Bishop 1990, 114).

In order to obtain a good job soon after entering the labor force, most young people find that they must pursue some form of postsecondary education. Of course, many people who lack postsecondary education eventually do obtain better positions (Edwards 1976). But the employers who give good jobs to applicants with limited educational credentials typically want a considerable amount of job experience; usually, they will not give such jobs to recent graduates. According to the Commission on the Skills of the American Workforce (1990, 46): "Few large firms in the United States will employ students who have just graduated from high school, preferring to wait until they have established some sort of track record elsewhere. . . . The result is that typical high school graduates mill about in the labor market, moving from one dead-end job to another until the age of 23 or 24. Then with little more in the way of skills than they had at eighteen, they move into the regular labor market."[9]

There are exceptions. Some school-based skills, such as word processing and mechanics, have an immediate use. Moreover, some firms require a somewhat higher level of literacy or numeracy from recent high school graduates. Large employers in Illinois were upset because high school graduates could not write a correct English sentence, and 15 percent of the large companies surveyed by the Commission on the Skills of the American Workforce reported occupation-specific shortages.

Not so long ago, large firms could use the high school diploma as a screen for many medium-level openings in clerical and production worker categories. Some of them would like to continue to make relatively good jobs available to recent graduates but complain that a diploma no longer signifies the level of cognitive achievement which it once did. Moreover, technological change in a number of these companies has raised the level of achievement needed by their work forces. The average youth with a high school diploma today who applies to these companies does not meet their standards. Some employers have increased use of their own tests, despite affirmative action concerns. These employers have often taken leading roles in the popular campaigns for educational reform of the 1980s and early 1990s.

Longer-Term Earnings Gains

Nevertheless, high school graduates who enter the labor force do achieve marked improvements in their economic positions, especially in the first decade or two of labor market experience. Annual earnings of graduates in their thirties are more than double the earnings of those just out of school, with some earning much more than that and some considerably less. Moreover, there are important changes in their earnings status relative to one another.

A variety of explanations have been put forward for these labor market dynamics. Economists who favor human capital arguments stress the importance of on-the-job experience in increasing the productivity of young people. Beginning jobs vary greatly: they may provide formal on-the-job training or more informal opportunities to develop one's capacities while at work (and, hence, one's earnings in later life). Individuals vary in their abilities to profit from these opportunities. Human capital theory predicts that young people with superior abilities or work ethics have a strong incentive to make investments in themselves by taking jobs that—although they may pay less initially, impose more stress, or afford less leisure time in the present—offer advancement. The argument is that the cognitive and social skills mastered in school make it easier to learn while on the job, so that the time spent in training will be more profitable. Moreover, as one rises from entry-level jobs to more complex situations, those with higher levels of verbal and mathematical achievements as well as social skills are favored. This provides an additional incentive for the more able to strive for advancement.

A complementary explanation emphasizes the role of information. The "matching theory" implies that, if employers begin with very little information about new graduates, the abilities of recent hires will only be revealed during the course of their employment. They can then move to more appropriate positions or can obtain a good reference and change employers. According to this theory, young people may gradually find the job in which their personal productivity will be highest.[10] These processes also help to explain why "general intellectual achievement" tends to pay off better in the long run than in the short run.

Effects of Long-Term Payoffs on the Incentive to Study

The failure of academic achievement in high school to bring short-term rewards in the labor market goes a long way toward explaining the low level of study effort of young Americans. When students know that their immediate success will be determined by how well they impress an employer during the hiring interview and that hard work at their first real job will produce more useful credentials than an above-average school performance, they have little incentive to study while in school.

The knowledge that academic achievement *may* be important in later life has little effect on the behavior of youngsters, who generally regard the time when they will be in their thirties, forties, and fifties as the very distant future and who know that, when they do become eligible for more desirable jobs some years hence, employers will still look at their prior job experience, rather than their high school records, in choosing to hire them or not. Employers will not care whether a high school graduate who is applying for a job that requires, say, ten years of full-time job experience was a B or a C student a decade earlier. Interestingly, this argument implies that, if students' academic achievement has any significant impact on their later labor market performance, it is because it raises their workplace *productivity*—that is, it has given them the literacy, numeracy, and social skills needed to handle more demanding jobs;[11] the grades they received are a secondary factor here.

Small wonder, then, that students ask whether it is really worth exerting the effort to produce what Michael Sedlak calls "surrogate credentials," his term for meaningless academic records.[12] Even if they take a long-term view and optimistically predict that they will eventually have better, more demanding jobs, this only gives them an incentive to study subjects that will be useful to a general business career, such as English or mathematics. When youngsters study other subjects (history or geography or some of the less relevant electives offered by high schools) simply to develop good credentials, it is not rational for them to study hard in these classes.

There is also a negative dialectic or spiral effect here. If the employer puts primary emphasis on socialization, best measured by the behavior of those who have recently left school, and if this behavior is not well reported by high schools, the employer will pay little attention to what high schools have to say about a student. If students learn that employers do not pay much attention to the signals, they will have less incentive to provide them; they will likely shirk, leading employers to pay still less attention to student behavior in making future employment decisions. A reasonable employer will expect youths to behave somewhat better in the adult world, where there are real incentives. The ultimate result is an equilibrium in which employers look only at whether young applicants have diplomas, and youths are demoralized by their experiences in school.

Chapter 6
Limiting Incentives at School

Children can be motivated in the educational system by small signs of approval, by praise, by good grades, and by special awards or the threat of not receiving these rewards. Passing to the next grade can be made a reward for achievement, rather than a birthright. Even retention in the classroom can be treated as a reward for behavior that meets the teacher's approval. Unfortunately, our public school system does *not* provide strong incentives to study. Moreover, it resists efforts by outsiders to force it to demand greater effort from students.

Albert Hirschman's (1970) classification of pressures on an institution as "exit" or "voice" is useful in understanding the U.S. educational system. According to Hirschman, pressures are exerted by the force of exit when individuals who participate in the activities of an organization (such as employees, stockholders, customers, suppliers, party members, or worshippers) leave it. Alternatively, the organization is pressured by voice when individuals use their influence, for example, through a trade union or suggestion box, to make their concerns known to management and thus effect change. Exit and voice influence decisions in corporations, political parties, trade unions, churches, and schools. Within the U.S. school system powerful voices oppose increased effort.[1]

Student Voices

Our analysis predicts that American students will not want to work very hard to get their diplomas because they will not see much payoff in the labor market for having devoted additional time to studying; they would rather be doing other things. Social scientists who spent thousands of hours observing U.S. classrooms confirm this view. Not only do individual students avoid study; their resistance typically extends to collective action. They know that, if they all work harder, the teacher will likely just "shift the curve," demanding more work for the same grade. The group imposes sanctions on classmates who work hard (e.g., by giving them derisive nicknames or excluding them from conversations), thus undermining the motivation of those who would otherwise be inclined to study.

The group can also impose sanctions on the teacher. In the typical U.S. high school classroom there is an unwritten "contract" between the teacher and students. The teacher does not demand very much work from them, and they, in turn, grant him or her a minimum of conventional respect. As Philip Cusick (1983, 53) put it, "Even if the students did not much care about learning abstract knowledge, they were still quite decent and had open, cordial relations with teachers." Teachers who violate the norm face serious difficulties. In addition to having an unpleasant classroom experience, they may face punishment by the principal for having poor relations with the students. As a result, according to Sedlak (1986, 2):

> [there is a] willingness to tolerate, if not encourage, diversion from the specified knowledge to be presented or discussed; the substitution of genial banter and conversation for concentrated academic exercises; improvisational instructional adaptation to student preference for or indifference toward specific subject matter or pedagogical techniques; the "negotiation" of class content, assignments, and standards; and a high degree of teacher autonomy.

This behavior is also found on the shop floor. For generations informal worker output restrictions have been described as "ca'canny," "soldiering on the job," "featherbedding," and a variety of other earthy epithets. In his book on school administration E. Mark Hanson (1979) points out that many of the group norms found in the pioneering Hawthorne studies of workers' behavior, conducted at the Western Electric Company in the early 1930s, can be seen today within student subcultures, including discouraging those who produce more than the group average. Modern labor economists call this shirking.

Students can also resist studying by taking easy courses, when it is permitted. This circumscribed form of exit affects tough teachers, who may lose students to those teaching less challenging classes. (The shop floor parallel here is inexact, since workers cannot always pick "easy" departments, and foremen are not rated according to how many workers they attract.)

Classroom contracts have their defenders (as do similar informal arrangements on the shop floor). They represent a shift in the control of student behavior from external forces (essentially, the teacher) to internal motivation, which organization theorists see as an advantage. The difference, says Hanson, "is the difference between treating people as children and treating them as mature adults" (85). In that context learning contracts between students and teachers are perceived as positive. As Hanson explains, "In entering into a learning contract with a teacher, the student gives definition to what he wants to learn, his methodology of learning (e.g., library, work book, visual aids), and how he wants his level of learning to be evaluated (e.g., written exam, term paper, or oral evaluation)" (86).[2] This argument is persuasive only if we accept the students' definition of the appropriate level of effort (a view that is critiqued in chap. 7).

Teacher Voices

Teachers often go along with, or at least compromise with, their students' efforts to reduce requirements. One explanation is that since "teachers depend on their students for much of their sense of success, accomplishment, and satisfaction," they must come to terms with what students desire to know (Sedlak 1986, 99). There are more objective reasons. School management does not support pushing students too hard, especially if it results in disruptive behavior or complaints from parents. Moreover, some instructors would rather not assign more work to students. Teachers often feel that they are already overworked, and increased student effort generally means that the teacher must work even harder. Preparing ambitious lesson plans is time consuming, as is assigning and grading homework. And the teacher is pressed for time. Many have children at home themselves; others moonlight at a second job. Moreover, in high schools that offer a specialized curriculum, a teacher often either is not well trained in the academic specialty or is required to teach outside of it.[3]

Critics argue that seniority and tenure provisions, as well as unionization,[4] foster a climate of limited effort. It is more difficult to dismiss lazy or incompetent teachers under these circumstances (Hanson 1979, 100–101). In the 1960s and 1970s teachers demanded and received greater autonomy. Critics maintain that some of them used their power to cut back on their work, designing courses that more closely fit their own capabilities and that were "fun" to teach. As a result, student effort was not encouraged. More sympathetic observers point to cases in which a relatively progressive managerial structure encouraged teachers to work hard, obtaining greater on-the-job satisfaction for themselves while helping students to learn.[5]

Shirking by Students and Teachers:
The Response of School Management

The prevalence of shirking in our public schools requires explanation. If a company's workers and foremen were the ones to make decisions about the appropriate level of employee effort, we might question the likelihood that it would survive. How is it that in our schools students and their teachers play such a large part in determining how much effort should be made?

Direct responsibility for shirking rests with the principals and other school administrators who permit or encourage the practice, since they are aware of classroom compromises and impose sanctions on teachers who violate them. Moreover, administrators develop the school's curriculum and can use this power to keep requirements low. Administrators have over the past thirty years altered curriculum requirements to allow students a great deal of choice. Even within the required core curriculum students often have a choice among courses; for example, a student can choose a relatively unchallenging English course whose name sounds quite like another, more demanding course. In this and other ways school administrators can control the flow of information about a student's learning or behavior. They can engage in what Oliver Williamson (1980), writing about imperfect information flows in large organizations, calls "opportunistic" behavior. Presenting patently inferior curricula as approximately the same as academically superior programs, so that a maximum number of graduates can be offered as suitable candidates for college admission or for employment, is an obvious example. Grade inflation can also be considered a form of opportunistic behavior because it helps principals to appease poor or lazy students and their parents.

Similarly, school principals can set up a track for relatively high-ability students in which work is at the level an outside observer would regard as satisfactory. Students who are not quite so able, yet whose parents act aggressively on their behalf, typically can obtain admission to this track. The principal thus satisfies the parents of industrious students without significantly increasing the overall level of demands on students. The career success of principals is largely determined by their ability to manage such short-run problems.[6]

Efforts over the last several years to reform education have had some impact here. States have insisted that curricular requirements be tightened in the weakest districts; some schools have set minimal achievement requirements for graduation; and some districts insist that teachers must also pass a test. Moreover, publication of district-wide data on National Assessment of Educational Progress (NAEP) scores has been useful in alerting parents to disparities among students and school systems. The overall pace of change has been disappointing, however.

Structural Resistance to Quality Improvements

This discussion still does not answer the real question: Why have we allowed such situations to develop and persist? Why has there been so little real reform? After all, school principals are public employees, not independent economic agents.

Some fault the institutional structure. Public K–12 education in the United States is owned and operated by local governments, subject to external constraints by state and federal governments and by the judiciary. Local governments are democratically elected—in many communities the school board is elected directly—and school principals correctly regard themselves as employees of a larger organization who may move up or down within it. Characteristic of such systems, its critics argue, is resistance to efforts to raise quality:

- The system favors increasing numbers of students, because school budgets are typically based on the number of students currently in attendance (Hanson 1979). A major criterion for evaluating a high school is the percentage of students graduating from it. Principals with high dropout rates caused by tough standards may risk losing their jobs.

- The system undervalues quality. According to Hanson (1979, 160), "The resource input . . . of a school system is not tied to the quality of its output . . . a sound argument can be made that there is an inverse relationship." If a school can show that its graduates are deficient, it can get more money; for example, "bond issues are usually passed when the quality of a program is declining."

- The system thinks in the short term. Raising standards for the present generation of students does bring benefits to future generations, as the reputation of the school improves, but the principal and school board must deal with the parents of the present generation, who are more concerned about their own children now. Even small groups of parents (or sometimes even a single parent) can cause considerable grief for a principal who raises effort requirements. A low rating now (due to dissatisfied parents) may be much more important to a school principal's career path than would better job prospects for graduates of the school five or ten years hence.

Lessons from Private Schools

Two prominent advocates of school choice, John Chubb and Terry Moe (1990, 31–32), believe many educational problems derive from our system of locally controlled, government schools.[7] The problem, they say, is not that the school system is too responsive to the demands of students and their parents. On the contrary, parents and children are only one set of actors on this stage. Politicians, administrators, teacher unions, professional associations, book publishers, ideological groups, and "factions among the citizens at large" all try to influence outcomes. Some win, some lose. This is not some accident or epiphenomenon. "The most fundamental point to be made about parents and students," according to Chubb and Moe, "is that, even in a perfectly functioning democratic system, the public schools are *not meant* to be theirs to control and are literally *not supposed* to provide them with the kind of education they might want."

Under our system, "in the public sector, the raison d'être of democratic control is to limit [the school's] autonomy." The schools have multiple "owners"—officials at the federal, state, and local levels—all under pressure from organized groups and constituents to use their authority. They have no choice but to execute hierarchical control over the schools, sharply limiting the schools' autonomy. But because of the "bottom-heavy nature of education technology," that is, the difficulty of controlling what actually goes on in the classroom from afar and the difficulty of measuring school performance, "outsiders, especially at the state and federal levels are compelled to issue and to endeavor to enforce a series of heavy-handed regulations." Thus, argue Chubb and Moe, "[the] root problem is not the bureaucrats, it is the causes of bureaucracy" (31–32).

The authors ask us to compare the private school management styles and academic performance with those of our public schools.[8] Within the private school the principal is a leader, not a lower-level management employee. He or she develops a coherent policy, with teachers working together as a team to advance a school's goals. "Parents and students are thrust onto center stage along with owners and staff. The rest of society plays a distinctly secondary role" (ibid.). Paradoxically, while parents have a vote in the public school system, and none in the private school, the former is influenced by a number of competing goals, the latter largely by an interest in attracting and keeping students.

Moreover, the owner-managers of the private school (like those in a more conventional small business) have an incentive to take a long-term view. They will benefit from gradually managing to improve the prospects for graduates by setting stricter standards, offsetting the pain of dealing with disgruntled parents who object to tougher standards now.

Private schools have a greater incentive to produce clear signals about their graduates. There is always some incentive to blur signals, especially with relatively weak students, but these schools must highlight their strengths in order to survive and grow. This provides an incentive to present information to employers and colleges which the latter will actually use. This constraint greatly reduces the payoff to private schools that behave opportunistically. Such behavior will always pay off in the very short run. To take an extreme example, if the graduates of a school have achieved an average grade of C for a long time, the principal can adjust the grading scale and give this year's graduates an advantage by awarding A grades to all, but employers and others will soon discount the school's records. They will either systematically readjust them back so that they give a more realistic reading of students' abilities and achievements or simply treat them as information of little or no value, turning instead to competing schools for graduates. If a school is judged by its longer-term success in placing students (rather than by its skill in dealing with students, parents, and other community groups), the gains from opportunistic behavior are sharply reduced.

Private schools also have a greater incentive to collect and disseminate accurate information about students because, as private institutions, they do not have to accept all applicants, graduate all students, or present all graduates as worthwhile candidates for employment. Hence, they can afford to be more forthcoming about the quality of their students. Moreover, if a certain school appeals to a specialized group of students, its communication about the students' credentials and the quality of their education is greatly simplified: employers know what schools to look to for a particular type of student, and principals have just one (or a few) products to market.

The less heterogeneous makeup of students within private schools can also simplify the educational process. The education of devoted, law-abiding students need not be disrupted by thugs or otherwise unmotivated students. More subtle advantages also can be obtained in more specialized schools. Large U.S. cities have long maintained a number of schools that specialize in science, music, or the arts, often with very good results.

This summary is not an argument for changing to a private system; our private schools also have their critics (see chap. 10). Looking at private schools does, however, highlight the problems of our public schools and hence the poor study effort of students.

The Force of the Status Quo

Once we understand that the public school system is biased toward larger enrollments, sometimes at the expense of quality; gets greater resources when quality drops; emphasizes short-term over long-term objectives; lacks incentives to produce good information about students; is hampered by having to deal with heterogenous student bodies; and is forced to respond to a variety of bureaucratic and political pressures rather than the needs of the families it serves, its often mystifying behavior becomes clearer.[9] Obviously, our school system is performing poorly, but why haven't we reformed the system?

Part of the answer is that the constituency for reform is reduced because young people prefer less study effort and because the labor market does not appropriately reward study. If we put a sufficiently high value on education for its own sake, these obstacles could largely be overcome. Many Americans, however, question whether an understanding of the so-called high culture really contributes to individual happiness—or, at least, whether the gain is worth the time and effort needed to acquire it.[10]

Where high cultural values are discounted, secondary and higher education is valued more pragmatically, primarily in terms of the practical advantages it will afford the child in later life, especially in the economic sphere. If a suitably disguised curriculum can enable a child to get into some college or community college, or at least enable him or her to enter the job market upon graduation with a marketable diploma, then it seems reasonable for local administrators to avoid all the unpleasantness that raising effort requirements would create.

Demands for change are also deflected because our school system serves political and bureaucratic interests, such as school system employees afraid of losing their jobs if the system becomes more competitive, minority groups fearful that members will perform poorly if school standards are raised, and many others who believe (rightly or wrongly) that they are benefiting under the present system. Finally, even those who demand reform do not agree about proposed "solutions," the types of changes which will put the system back on track.[11]

Cumulative Effects of School System and Labor Market Failures

The various system failures cited here interact to discourage study effort. For example, if school reform ideas are judged by how well they contribute to the economic success of graduates, the practical problems of measuring the earnings payoff to study effort become an important obstacle. Similarly, while the superficial use of school credentials by employers encourages principals to tolerate low standards and confusing transcripts, the failure of schools to supply good information has made employers skeptical of the little information they do obtain.

As skepticism among employers increases, the motivation of children to study and the schools' incentive to crack down on lazy students are both weakened. The net result of these interactions is that students have little incentive not to shirk. Too often, rather than learning the good work habits and attitudes toward authority which would make them more effective employees,[12] their school experience convinces them that group-oriented ca'canny pays off, that insolence to a superior can be a virtue, that hard work does not pay, and that goofing off on the job is the norm—and a comfortable norm at that. Such negative effects further reduce the value of high school education to the employer, who can only hope that the youth will "shape up" in the real world of adult employment.

The result is that most American parents tell pollsters that, while they are well satisfied with the public school their children attend, they believe that the U.S. public school system is in terrible shape.

III THE NEED FOR CHANGE

Chapter 7

Should We Care? The Role of Social Policy

If the behavior of our young people is rational and maximizes their utility, should it concern the rest of society? And even if it does, is legislation the best remedy? The answers may seem obvious today, but this was not always the case. Attitudes toward student effort, and, more generally, toward the educational progress of our young people, have shifted in recent years.

As recently as the 1950s, the dominant view in the United States was that we should educate our children for life. "Life adjustment skills," including proficiency in interpersonal relations, were stressed, often at the expense of cognitive achievement (Toch 1991). Critics of this attitude occasionally were heard, as when a national poll found that 40 percent of U.S. high school students believed that the earth was the center of the universe (Sedlak 1986, 18) or when the public learned that a large number of students did not know the name of the Atlantic Ocean. The more common view, however, was that most schools were doing a satisfactory job.

The launch of Sputnik in 1957 by the Soviet Union challenged our complacency and focused attention on the comparatively low level of achievement of our students, especially in mathematics and science. The civil rights movement of the early 1960s directed attention to the very poor education received by most black children in the United States, providing further argument for an upgrading of standards. In the same period economists launched the human capital theory, which endeavored to explain most of the variation in earnings among individuals as a function of education, training, and other investments made in them. For all these reasons, by the late 1960s interest in education peaked.

In the 1970s less emphasis was placed on academic achievement. Schools were attacked as undemocratic or elitist (a view often supported by civil rights and student activists). Schools were often saddled with new social responsibilities, along with their conventional function of instructing students. Teachers in many schools were urged to devote more time to the less able in their classrooms and to be more tolerant of disruptive behavior. Economists themselves retreated from the human capital explanations of earnings differentials. Some placed more emphasis on the newly developed signaling and screening theories. Others looked for the causes of earnings differentials on the demand side, in theories of segregated labor markets, in which lucky graduates were permitted to work their way up in an internal labor market (such as that provided by a profession, an organized craft structure, or a large corporation), while others, often minority youths, were trapped in the more casual "secondary labor market," without much hope of upward mobility (Doeringer and Piore 1971; Gordon, Edwards, and Reich 1982). Reputable economists argued that we were overeducating our young people, relative to the available job opportunities, and it is true that the return to college education declined temporarily (Freeman 1975). Some went so far as to argue, using an extreme version of the screening theory, that increasing education for all young people need not either raise productivity or reduce inequality.[1]

In the 1980s, spurred by international competition, schools again came under fire for their poor job of educating the young. A blizzard of studies, reports, and commission findings demanded change, but actual reform efforts proceeded slowly against substantial opposition. While many agree that some change would be a good idea, there is little consensus on more than a handful of improvements. Defenders of the status quo believe that our system represents American values; that demands for change rely on unproved hypotheses; and that proposed innovations would be divisive, costly, and harmful.

At this impasse we may ask whether economic analysis offers any grounds for advocating government policies that could reform the system. The question is *not* whether we should approve students' participation in a costly and time-consuming youth culture at the expense of their serious study in school. The question is, rather, whether correcting this situation is an appropriate task for public policy. Most economists would very likely share the common opinion that apathetic student behavior is unfortunate, but they would refrain from recommending government intervention unless certain well-known criteria for an active policy are met.

Government intervention may be justified in certain cases: when there are externalities, that is, social benefits that are not properly rewarded in the marketplace;[2] when there are macroeconomic effects, such as a change in economic growth; when individuals discount the future at a rate that is higher than that preferred by society; or when there is strong reason for believing that society is in a better position to make a rational judgment than is the individual. Many economists would add cases in which income is redistributed from richer to poorer citizens.[3] Each case is relevant to the question of study effort.

The first case has a long tradition. The social benefits of education were stressed before Adam Smith's day, and they are still an important consideration today.[4] A better-schooled population generally makes for a well-informed, more active electorate that takes care of its health and provides a stronger basis for transmitting the national culture. This is the sort of argument traditionally used to support public subsidies for education.

Promoting Economic Growth

In the 1990s the argument for educational reform is most typically based on its contribution to economic growth. Education contributes to growth by increasing the effective labor force, among other things. The effective supply of labor is determined by the total number of hours supplied and by the quality of labor. Education improves the quality dimension insofar as useful skills and habits are learned in school and employed in the workplace. If we accept the idea that, on average, wage rates are a rough measure of productivity, then the effect of an increase in education on productivity can be measured by the increase in wage rates that results. For example, if a college education raises the wage rates of graduates by 30 percent, then an increase of 10 percent in the proportion of college graduates would represent a 3 percent increase in the effective labor force (if hours of work are not affected by the change in wage rates).[5]

This class of benefits, raising the contributions of the work force, is not a strong candidate for state intervention, though increased labor supply does benefit the rest of society: in addition to the higher earnings of employees supplying more labor, employers and taxpayers also benefit. As more labor, or better-quality labor, is available for employment in offices and factories, business profits will rise. In some economic models profits rise in roughly the same proportion as labor earnings.[6] Moreover, since both business and labor pay taxes on their earnings, government benefits from a larger effective labor force, receiving more tax revenue because of it. While these benefits are well-known,[7] they are not generally regarded as suitable grounds for government action.

Tax revenues and business profits would both likely increase if we reverted to a six-day workweek, but few advocate minimum working time legislation.[8] Far from being a source of social concern, U.S. leaders have long pointed to our reduced work schedules with pride. The shorter workweek and the annual vacations that Americans enjoy are regarded as major accomplishments of our capitalist system. This positive attitude toward the leisure of adults raises an interesting question: How can we justify criticizing the low level of study effort of our young people, or that combination of leisure time and part-time work which yields our internationally famous youth culture, when as adults we cherish our own leisure activities? The low level of study effort does lower the quality of our labor force, and this, in turn, leads to a less productive economy. But is it really any more costly than the two-day weekend?

There is a much stronger case to be made here for improving the educations of those entering the labor force: a better educated work force facilitates a more rapid rate of technological change. Jacob Mincer (1984, 206) explains the argument this way:

> Educational activities . . . involve not only the transmission and embodiment in people of available knowledge but also the production of new knowledge, which is the source of innovation and technological change . . . creating national and worldwide economic growth. . . . Consequently, estimates of effects of education on economic growth are understated if they confine themselves to effects on the quality of labor and leave out the effects on technological change.[9]

Technological improvement is defined as an increase in output with all other inputs—labor, capital, materials, energy, and so on—held constant. A major factor in the rising living standards, over the long run, of individuals at each education level has been technical change. Moreover, if a change in the rate of technical progress, rather than a onetime increase in technology, can be achieved, the long-term effects will be far-reaching, indeed. Compound interest comes into play, so that even a relatively small increase, say 1 percent per year, will have profound implications over a period of ten, twenty, or thirty years. Conversely, a slowdown in growth rates also has profound effects. Slow growth rates since the mid-1960s have had strongly negative effects on U.S. society. People complain that the generation now entering the labor force is the first that has not done better than the one before.[10] In a world in which capital is increasingly mobile and technical change has accelerated, many believe that high capital-labor ratios, and hence relatively high-paying jobs, are only found where the work force can easily adjust to the rapid adaptation of new technology.[11]

Noneconomists, especially those who reflect the views of the business community, make these arguments in less abstract terms. The U.S. business community is doing a first-rate job of presenting the argument for educational reform as an appropriate agenda for government policy.[12] The business community is the principal market for the school's products, so we should listen when it demands an upgrading of the product. Its publications predict that in the absence of change the United States will stagnate, as the "good jobs" move to find a work force that can adapt to innovations, leaving us with the "bad," or unskilled, jobs. Not only will our living standards decline but the ability of the nation's leaders to influence international events, and more generally its prestige and status, will suffer. Such "public goods" are, indeed, traditional objects of government policy.

Effects of Student Effort on Economic Growth

There is no debate about whether an increase in years of schooling raises earnings and productivity.[13] It is more difficult to make these connections in terms of student effort. The earnings gains from increased study while in school are very small for young people. Yet there is reason to believe that study effort increases scholastic achievement and that this achievement, in turn, increases productivity. Pay may not vary much with the cognitive achievement of young people, but productivity does.

Recent research indicates that the productivity of young employees is positively related to their scores on a measure of scholarly attainment, implying that the contribution to economic growth of academic achievement is not accurately reflected in wages (see Bishop 1987, 1989c, 1992). Employers generally do not bother to sort out young employees carefully, and, when they do, they do not always institute meaningful pay differentials. It takes resources to sort out workers, and, because the turnover rate is high, it doesn't pay. Moreover, in addition to direct sorting costs, employers might feel that pay differentials for employees working side by side create bad feelings between them and lower morale. Further, some employers believe their employees should understand that productivity will be rewarded in the future (by retention and by promotion within the firm, for example, or by a good letter of reference if they leave), so it should not be necessary to offer immediate rewards such as better wages (ibid.).

Earnings returns on an individual's achievement get better in subsequent years. Insofar as this reflects a sorting process in the labor market, with those who are more accomplished being assigned to more appropriate tasks, these later returns might be a fairer measure of their contribution than what we see in the wages they earn when they first join the labor force. Perhaps the most persuasive argument for the view that achievement is the principal factor explaining the relationship between education and growth is the weakness of the alternative hypothesis: Can education and economic growth be related only through diplomas and other paper credentials? (See Wolpin 1977.)

Future research, with better data, may be able to demonstrate that cognitive achievement and socialization skills, *not* years of schooling as such, are relevant to U.S. competitiveness. In the meantime policymakers might be well advised to assume that the business community accurately understands the deficiency in skills of the U.S. work force in the context of today's technology.

The Social Cost of Student Effort

Assume that the benefits of economic growth are obtained as readily by more study each year as by more years. Then consider the likely lower social costs of increasing effort. Increased years of schooling require sacrificing output. There is a net gain only insofar as the future improvement in the quality of labor will outweigh the costs of keeping the labor of students, teachers, administrators, and other employees out of the production of investment or consumer goods.[14] In contrast, increased study effort would mean that students must sacrifice a portion of their leisure time and work more intensively while in class. Many students would have to give up their part-time jobs. In addition, there may be direct costs to the taxpayers. When school days and years are extended, teachers typically demand that their salaries be increased. Operating costs—for heating, cooling, security, and so forth—also increase when schools are open longer.

These adjustments are almost trivial, however, in comparison to the costs imposed by the present system of raising cognitive achievement by increasing years of schooling, so that many students learn material in expensive colleges which they could have learned in the K–12 grades. When these costs are taken into account, a policy designed to increase study effort will most likely be seen to have a larger net effect on economic growth than a policy developed to increase years of schooling. [15]

Another reason to reject a laissez-faire approach to the degree of student effort is that students in the K–12 levels are children. Few economists would argue that decisions made by children should be the basis for public policy; after all, children tend to heavily discount the future, to be poorly informed about their own needs and those of society, and to lack emotional maturity. This is not to say that the leisure of children and adolescents is valueless but, rather, that youngsters typically place a higher value on their present leisure than do their parents or the rest of society.

Government Policies Now Limit Effort

Perhaps the strongest economic case for a government policy on student effort derives from the fact that in the United States public schools are already administered by the state. One does not have to debate the merits of government ownership or control. [16] Policy in the public schools is now determined by the government—actually, by a wide variety of government initiatives, including federal, state, and local legislation as well as court rulings. The present debate centers on whether to replace one set of directives with another, more satisfactory set. [17]

To take an example of a de facto policy directive, our present school system offers schooling free to young people while imposing very lax rules for remaining in school, thus minimizing the reward for their effort while there. Students have a powerful incentive to substitute the duration of schooling (which has few out-of-pocket costs) for effort while in school (which they want to avoid). Our educational system imposes a large financial burden: K–12 schooling costs taxpayers several hundred billion dollars a year. We know that the positive outputs of schools (cognitive achievement and socialization) are functions of both number of years in school and the youth's study effort while there. A system that subsidizes duration but not effort will therefore yield less achievement than would a more balanced subsidy policy. [18] It is, therefore, unlikely that we are obtaining the maximum educational gain for our tax dollars.

A policy of subsidizing duration poorly serves what might be called "the rest of society," taxpayers without children or whose children are not in school. If a student's time and effort while in school (which costs the taxpayer nothing) were substituted for duration of schooling (which costs the taxpayer a lot), educational goals could be achieved at a lower cost to taxpayers, who have seen their positions deteriorate under the present policy of ever longer hours of schooling, accompanied by an apparent reduction in effort while there. The American student now has a pleasant time while in school and plenty of free time in the afternoons and evenings. The taxpayer's burden continues to grow. The interests of taxpayers and students on the effort-duration issue are at loggerheads.

Chapter 8

Borrowing from Abroad

How Other Countries Obtain More Study Effort

There is a continuing effort to disparage the accomplishments of our competitors, as when foreign students are said to learn through memorization and so do not achieve the habit of independent or critical thinking or when we are told that homogeneous societies do not have to design a multicultural curriculum. Such statements do not give an accurate picture of our competitors' accomplishments. Factual knowledge is required in the study of science, history, geography, and foreign languages. Even in subjects regarded as basic "tools for learning," such as mathematics or one's own language, students learn a number of useful facts, such as how words are spelled or how to add numbers.[1] The acquisition of factual knowledge depends on memorization.

Yet learning in successful foreign systems is not based simply on memorization. Even in Japan, high school mathematics examinations require students to work out complex, multistage problems whose solution demands a great deal of critical thinking.[2] Moreover, the submissiveness or lack of initiative abroad which some Americans report may result from a different notion of creative behavior in other countries. When comparing European and American students at the college level, Edmund King (1967, 203) points out that "foreign professors generally find American students too docile for their taste. More importance is attached to final grades and 'credit hours' than to searching examination or critical reading as expected of students everywhere outside North America." The difference may stem from the common practice there of giving as homework a "textbook assignment that must be read and thoroughly assimilated for discussion in the next day" (27).

Clearly, observers from other cultures will perceive our system differently. What an American may regard as healthy behavior by adolescents in the course of "finding themselves" might strike someone from another country as inappropriate classroom comportment.[3]

Finally, while schools in the United States are wrestling with the problem of establishing a curriculum that is culturally diverse, the Japanese have long insisted that their students study the Western canon (so despised by academic radicals in this country). In Japanese textbooks on ethics and society, according to Thomas Rohlen (1983, 257), European thought "from its Greek and Christian origins to its recent products . . . receives the most attention." There is a "predominance of Western over Eastern thinkers." Moreover, in texts on world history "more than half the pages are devoted to European and American history."

Of course, one should not expect to find problem-free utopias elsewhere. According to a recent study by the Brookings Institution, "there is not a single industrial nation that is not dissatisfied with the quality of the product of its education and worker training systems" (Nothdurft 1989, 4). Foreign observers, in fact, often find some features of American education attractive. Nevertheless, we do have something to learn from foreign examples. To this end, let us first consider some significant characteristics of the more successful nations, then consider whether they can be imported into our own system.

Strong Family and Social Support

In most of the nations competing with us, a positive attitude toward study is strongly supported by the student's family. Typically, the media presents a positive image of scholarly youths. Japanese families instill a positive attitude toward study effort even in preschool-age children and continue to encourage it throughout the school years. In other successful nations the family, while not reaching Japanese levels of support, still takes a more positive attitude toward study than does the typical American family (King 1967).[4] In addition, the popular culture in these countries is not openly hostile to study effort.

In many of the countries competing with us, a modern educational system developed as part of a concerted effort to create a unified, industrial nation. The school system was designed to raise the technical accomplishments of students while at the same time transmitting national values and culture to the new generations, in the face of rapid economic and social change (King 1967; Nothdurft 1989; Rohlen 1983).

Close Relations between Schools and Employers

According to William Nothdurft (1989, 5), in recent years some countries of Western Europe, particularly Germany and Sweden, "saw that the secret to securing larger export market share was product quality—specifically, workers with relevant skills." As a result, "integration of the world of school and the world of work, already advanced in these countries, has accelerated during the past decade."[5]

In most West European countries there is now a strong support system for *all* students (Grant Foundation 1988; King 1967; Nothdurft 1989). Those who are not college bound but who otherwise have a satisfactory record are singled out early for apprenticeships, vocational education, placement, or other assistance leading to long-term, productive, relatively well-paid positions. This European system benefits working-class youths directly, by improving their job prospects, and indirectly, by bolstering morale. Low morale depresses the study effort of Americans who know that they are not college bound.[6] The benefits to employers are obvious.

There is, too, a much better flow of information between schools and employers in Western Europe. Employers are given more information about student records and use these data in their hiring decisions. School and work are integrated through work-study programs that give employers information about potential employees.

Our competitors typically offer longer-term employment relationships to youngsters just leaving school. In contrast, young Americans usually work at a number of short-term jobs before settling into a more stable job (Commission on the Skills of the American Workforce 1990, 46). When employers hire long-term employees directly from school, they have a far greater incentive to concern themselves with the applicant's high school record, and this increases incentives to perform well in school.

National or Regional Examinations

The other developed nations use national or regional examinations to measure learning—achievement, not aptitude. In some countries such exams are administered to youths in their early teens and the results used to determine their subsequent training or schooling. Results from examinations taken just before graduation are passed along to employers. The exam score itself becomes a marketable credential, almost as important as the diploma. The result is much more learning as well as much more study effort.

While national examinations have some drawbacks—some students will suffer excessive anxiety, for example, while teachers may feel that they are constrained to "teach to the test"—they offer a number of advantages. For one thing, they discourage Mickey Mouse curricula. Moreover, everyone learns that deliberately mislabeling courses is counterproductive: if a course labeled twelfth-grade English does not prepare a person for the senior year examination in English, it is not likely to be very popular with students. These tests expose lazy or incompetent teachers, while undercutting the rationale for classroom contracts. In Japan high school teachers encourage their students to regard national examinations as an opportunity for them to work together to raise the performance of the entire class.

In some successful countries a common curriculum is rigorously enforced by a central educational authority. While this practice has obvious disadvantages, it does make it easier to study for a standardized examination and may reduce inequality in achievement, by eliminating what Chester Finn (1991, 219) calls "curriculum tracking," that is, watering down course content for students judged less able.

Japan, France, Great Britain, and many other countries allow a student to apply to a number of high schools (King 1967; Rohlen 1983). The desire to be admitted to the school of one's choice provides a strong incentive for junior high school students to study hard. In these systems academic requirements for college admissions are higher, but well-prepared students can often go to excellent universities on full scholarships, including room and board. This provides a major incentive to scholastic achievement at the high school level.

The basic difference between us and our competitors relates to incentives. Overall, in these countries, there is a much better flow of information from schools to employers; a sense of a national mission which motivates the schools; and a less supportive attitude toward the leisure of children. The effects are heavy coursework, homework, long days and years, even for those not going beyond high school, and still more intense pressure on those with greater academic ambitions. There is little of the youth culture seen in the United States. And people leave school with significantly greater cognitive achievement as well as much lower delinquency rates.

Chapter 9

Can Our Schools Demand More Effort?

There are two, complementary methods for improving student effort: changing the educational process directly, by forcing schools to demand more effort, or changing the external environment, by giving schools greater incentives to demand study effort and students greater incentives to supply it.

The attempts by nations to improve the quality of their industrial products provides a useful analogy. In the United States market forces are dominant, and industries are forced to adapt to pressures for improved quality. In response to overseas competition, U.S. manufacturers are now engaged in a sustained endeavor to match Japanese quality levels by carefully monitoring the production process, "building quality in," at every stage. A very high standard of "zero defects" is set and adhered to.

Current reform efforts in Russia exemplify a second useful method. The former USSR did not have a market economy in our sense, with the result that factories and other enterprises lacked appropriate incentives to improve quality. Western economists agree that necessary first steps toward raising quality require a major restructuring of society, with the eventual result that managers and workers will find it in their own interest to see that what they produce meets a reasonable standard.

The first method improves quality through control of the production process, while the second improves it by restructuring institutions so that they offer individual rewards for good performance. The two methods complement each other.

Building in Quality

Although people cannot be compared to automobile parts, one can think of ways to build quality into our educational process as factories have done. The educational systems and related institutions can be restructured to increase incentives for schools to turn out quality products.

Widely advocated educational reforms designed to build quality into our school system include:

- Tightening up the curriculum by introducing and requiring a common core of subjects to be studied (Clune 1989; Firestone 1989).

- Sharply increasing "time on task" in class, that is, the time actually spent teaching, by: lengthening the school day and year; enforcing attendance and tardiness rules; insisting on classroom discipline; reducing interruptions of class periods for administrative purposes; and establishing better priorities within the class period, so that essential topics receive the most attention.[1]

- Requiring more homework outside of class.

- Replacing the social pass system with merit passes in schools that still pass all students.

- Requiring appropriate student behavior in class. The goal here is to change behavior or at least to separate disruptive students from those who want to learn. This can include using sanctions against poorly disciplined children, keeping minor offenders after school, and separating major offenders by transferring them to special schools.

- Tracking within schools by achievement or assigning unusually able students to specialized schools. Some form of tracking is now found in many of our secondary schools. Advocates of tracking argue that it permits schools to offer able students a more demanding curriculum, increasing their effort and achievement. Opponents believe, however, that tracking weakens the educations of those who are not designated as able, in part because their teachers have lower expectations of them. Empirical research evaluating these claims yields mixed results.[2]

The adoption of these reforms could, in principle, significantly improve the achievement level of young Americans. Yet there are serious obstacles to change. Hirschman's (1970) exit/voice paradigm is again useful in helping to classify these difficulties. Students can resist tougher requirements by exit, either by dropping out of school or by refusing to conform to school rules, forcing the system to expel them. A reduction in the proportion that finishes a given number of years of school, of course, conflicts with the widely accepted goals of raising high school completion rates and increasing the number of college students.[3] This conflict limits our ability to deal with low student effort by raising requirements.

Economists would recognize the problem as one of making an economic choice: an unsatisfactorily low level of achievement by graduates or an unsatisfactorily low number of graduates. The optimal solution requires a tradeoff between longer number of years spent in school and more effort while in school. It depends on two things: how we predict the change in termination rates resulting from changes in effort requirements (called here "student reaction functions") and how policymakers weigh improved quality of graduates against reductions in their number (called here "social objective functions").[4]

Student Reaction Functions

We assume that the average student prefers to make less effort in school than will be demanded, despite his or her knowledge that more effort now is likely to yield higher income and other benefits in later life.[5] We also assume that students prefer to stay in school longer rather than work hard while in school. The alternative to staying in school is either full-time employment or unemployment, and these may be as unattractive as school.[6] The alternative to homework time is more leisure, a more desirable activity for many young people. Moreover, because additional years of schooling are a more reliable route to higher earnings in the future, given a choice, many students opt for a low effort-duration ratio; that is, they would rather stay in school than work harder there.

This preference for staying in school can, up to a point, be used to induce students to work harder while in school, *if* their continued education is made conditional on a specified level of effort. But, if effort requirements rise sufficiently, they are likely to terminate schooling. *The higher the effort requirement, then, the higher the proportion dropping out.*

The student's preference for duration over effort is strengthened when, as in our public school system, school is free or almost free. Free instruction removes an incentive to acquire cognitive achievement quickly. *At the same time, subsidizing students' educations means that the school can demand more effort: if students do not supply the effort and leave school, they lose a bargain: cheap schooling.*[7]

Social Objective Functions

If policymakers' objectives are to maximize the number of students who graduate or, alternatively, simply to maximize the utility of students, then schools should demand the same low level of effort which students themselves would choose. A higher standard than that will increase the rate of terminations. If schools' objective is to increase the average level of educational attainment, they will impose a stricter rule, in which further gains in learning per year by those students who meet a higher standard are just offset by the loss of further education for those who fail to meet the more stringent requirement. Obviously, applying even this simple rule will produce different results, depending on how policymakers weigh the importance of dropouts relative to the excellence of graduates in calculating the average level of educational attainment.

Those who seek to maximize long-term economic growth will prefer a still stricter rule because they will include the cost of keeping youths in school. To estimate the effect of future national wealth, they will translate educational attainment or learning into future earnings gains, then compare these gains with the total costs of schooling.[8] Insofar as student effort in school is costless (or at least relatively cheap), while additional years in school are quite expensive, this criterion is expected to yield an effort-duration ratio that is higher than the one obtained when learning itself is maximized.

Finally, maximizing the interest of taxpayers implies a rule that requires students to make a greater effort in school than would be required by the rule followed to maximize growth. While taxpayers do obtain some benefit from growth, inasmuch as a portion of the earning increment due to education is returned to the government as tax revenue, graduates keep the larger portion for their own consumption.[9] Hence, a greater earnings gain per additional year of schooling is needed for taxpayers to obtain a net benefit from their subsidy. Taxpayers may, however, be somewhat more tolerant of low effort if they believe that further education means lower welfare incidence in the future.[10]

How Many Dropouts Can Be Tolerated?

Reasonable policymakers will differ about the best choice among tradeoffs between effort while in school and the length of time spent there, depending on whether they give the greatest weight to maximizing completion rates, educational achievement, economic growth, or minimizing the burden on taxpayers. Those more concerned with the social effects of an underclass of dropouts might want a lower level of terminations than those who argue that our work force must show more achievement to compete internationally. But the model presented here indicates that, with tougher requirements on study effort, some exit is likely, unless an extremely egalitarian policy is adopted.

How Do We Measure Effort?

Schools do not have reliable measures of student effort. They typically can measure a student's achievement, but achievement is the result of ability as well as effort. Because students vary in both ability and industry, and school systems lack full information about these individual characteristics, they can at best measure effort approximately. In principle they can calculate the change in achievement over a period of time, relative to the student's ability to achieve, and use the gain as a proxy for effort.

In practice this is a very difficult task. Moreover, individual scores show considerable variability from one year to the next; if a student has a "good day" on examination day in 1993 and a "bad day" when tested in 1994, his or her progress could be seriously underestimated.

A school might group students by their expected academic ability and then interpret differences in achievement among individuals in the group as reflecting differences in effort.[11] But this procedure is not very useful for policy purposes. Since any such grouping will be imperfect, some lower-ability students will be incorrectly classified as more able; if they are then held to a high standard of achievement, they are apt to fail to meet that standard and be terminated.

And, even if full information about student ability and effort were available to school systems, ability differences could still make it difficult for schools to insist on a high level of performance from all students. The more able students will resent being required to achieve more than those who are less capable simply to pass their courses and stay in school. Finally, for quite different reasons ability tracking has become increasingly controversial in our public school systems and is attacked in many school districts in which it is practiced.[12]

Yet the most powerful obstacle to higher requirements is the growing conviction among reformers that any reduction in the proportion of young people finishing high school is unacceptable. Instead, we must somehow *simultaneously* raise standards at each level of schooling and increase the number of years completed. This view is not necessarily limited to those who are ignorant of the problems caused by poor academic performance. For example, Gary Wehlage and Robert Rutter's review (1986, 381) of the social costs of keeping students in school concludes that, while still in high school, future dropouts are poor students, cut classes, and provide disciplinary problems for teachers and other students. "It may be that some kinds of children are more difficult to teach than others," they suggest, and then go on to say, "but the school has no less of a mandate to do its best to provide all the schooling that such children can profitably use."

This obstacle is more formidable insofar as higher requirements yield disproportionately high dropout rates for minority students and for those from low socioeconomic backgrounds. Since dropout rates are now highest for these groups, a serious social problem would be exacerbated if standards are raised (Ekstrom and others 1986).

Institutional Obstacles to Higher Standards

Resistance to higher academic standards is not limited to concerns over exiting by students. There is vocal resistance within the system. As noted earlier, principals and local school boards are unlikely to make the painful choices needed to raise academic standards unless they are accompanied by other reforms. Championing a policy that raised the failure and dropout rates in their schools would be political suicide for many of these officials.[13]

Tougher standards could be mandated at the federal rather than the local level, but voice operates here as well, in part through well-organized pressure groups that lobby on the national level. Moreover, the American tradition rejects micromanagement of the school system by the federal government and prefers to delegate control to local school boards and local and state governments.

In practice, raising effort requirements would likely require the cooperation of federal, state, and local systems. Such cooperation is unlikely, however, if increases in effort requirements cause school dropout rates to rise substantially: the political, social, and economic climate is not at all favorable for that development. Even during the 1980s, when public clamor led to the establishment of a number of national commissions to examine the low level of study effort and to propose solutions, and when states and localities initiated numerous reforms, effort requirements were not increased much. According to recent research, the major result was the strengthening of curriculum requirements in many of the weaker schools.[14] And in the 1990s we continue to press for lower dropout rates as well as greater effort.

An Insoluble Dilemma?

We thus appear to be confronted with unacceptable choices: either adopt policies that are sure to eliminate students or continue to allow a depressingly low level of student effort. The first is ruled out by a consensus that dropout rates must be reduced. The second is equally unacceptable if we are to be competitive. But, if neither course of action is acceptable, we must look for a way out of our dilemma.

There is much that the schools themselves can do to ameliorate the dropout problem: win-win solutions raise effort requirements while minimizing the increase in attrition. Extensive counseling services, tutoring, and other after-school assistance programs are typical suggestions. In addition, the education literature is full of innovative ideas for making schools more effective, "smarter," or more fun, so that more learning can occur in them without losing students. At the present time promising experiments are being conducted at a number of sites across the nation. The long history of educational reform movements, however, advises us to be cautious about quick-fix solutions. In the short run, at least, it seems that real choices have to be made.

The choices can at least be made less harsh if we are also willing to consider broader, though quite straightforward, changes in the school system. Consider how the labor market deals with personnel who will not or cannot achieve. Employees are held to a standard and are dismissed if they fail to meet it. Indeed, if the employee's record indicates that he or she is unlikely to meet company standards, the person will not be hired in the first place.[15] But rejection or dismissal by a company does not mean that the individual is ejected from the labor market. In most cases he or she finds work in a firm in which abilities and willingness to supply effort yield a level of performance which is regarded as satisfactory. Obviously, the existence of alternative opportunities for workers very much reduces the social cost of dismissing employees. If schools were organized in an analogous fashion, there would be a variety of schools, each offering different rewards. A student who was admitted to a school of higher quality but who was unwilling to supply the necessary effort to keep up with the work would be required to move to another, more appropriate institution, not simply lost to the system.

Our major European competitors have educational systems that approximate the labor market much more closely than does our own.[16] When German students reach the age of ten, they are divided into two groups on the basis of grades and teachers' recommendations. About one-third go to the Gymnasium, to prepare for university training. The remainder go to the Hauptschule.[17] At about age twelve those in Hauptschule can take another examination to enter either the Gymnasium or an intermediate school, the Realschule. At the age of nineteen Gymnasium students take an examination for admission to university. At the intermediate Realschule students take examinations at the age of sixteen or seventeen. They may then enter the university, go to a higher technical school (as many do), or enter an apprenticeship. The large bulk of students in the Hauptschule finish full-time schooling at age fifteen or sixteen; typically, they then begin an apprenticeship.

In all, two-thirds of German secondary school graduates enter the apprenticeship system. It produces workers skilled in both the theory and practice of their trade, learned on the job or in specialized training centers. During their apprenticeships youths spend at least one day a week in school. Apprenticeships are common even in the service industries, even in such disparate areas as banking and restaurant work, as well as in the traditional manufacturing industries.

At the end of a three-year apprenticeship the youths take two exams, a nationally administered written examination and a practical examination. If successful, the young man or woman becomes a journeyman and usually can find work in the appropriate field. The worker may continue going to school if he or she so chooses. After a minimum of three more years of work experience and courses in business management, law, and technology, the youth is eligible to take an examination to be certified as a "Master." Craftworkers must obtain this certificate before they can open a business. All this training, according to William Nothdurft (1989, 31–32), "builds confidence and self-esteem as carefully as it builds practical skills . . . [and] creates a pool from which many of the nation's middle managers are drawn."

Incentives are maintained throughout the system. Attractive technical schools are more demanding than others. Moreover, applications for apprenticeships in some occupations or firms (especially for those leading to better-paying positions) far exceed the number available. Competitive pressures thus provide incentives to study for those who know that they are not headed for a university. As a result, German educators are not faced with a choice between low requirements and ejecting children from the system. A student may enter a wide variety of subsystems. Those who hope to go to a university know that they will have to study hard at the secondary level (very hard, by American standards). And those who do not do so well in school are not relegated to our "forgotten half" but, instead, continue to have meaningful incentives to study and work.

This solution involves a significant restructuring of our educational system. Our present system resembles the German model in that our young people have a wide variety of options available to them upon graduation from high school: they can enter the labor force, go to a selective college that requires considerable effort, or attend a post-secondary institution that is somewhat less demanding, among other things. Yet applying the European system to the K–12 grades in this country would represent a major change, not at all an easy one to achieve.[18] Indeed, if *all* we proposed was to provide a set of less demanding schools for those who are doing poorly in their academic programs, the proposal might even be rejected as an attempt to impose an undemocratic system of tracking on young children.[19]

The next chapter considers the adoption of some features of the European system as part of a broader analysis of the second strategy for change, institutional reforms that offer students and schools greater incentives to improve.

Chapter 10

Creating Positive Incentives for Study

We have seen that the stick of higher effort requirements may be needed to obtain more work from students, but economic analysis indicates that the carrot of positive reinforcement will also be needed, and it will require complementary changes in the school system and, very likely, in the environment in which our schools operate as well.

Direct Financial Incentives

A simple, and superficially attractive, carrot is to pay students to study. Their salaries could vary with performance, on the basis of the same factors that teachers traditionally use to grade students: homework done neatly and on time, good class attendance and deportment, high scores on tests, and so on. This method is comparatively simple to introduce. Moreover, there are successful, if small-scale, precedents for them; many American parents give their children cash allowances that are dependent, in part, on good performance in school; philanthropists in a number of school districts now give large prizes to students who do well; and, of course, hope of a college scholarship has long stimulated the more able students to work harder.[1]

Large-scale use of cash payments by school systems or by outside parties is uncommon, however, in part because of the poor results when it was tried in the early decades of the nineteenth century. In order to provide an inexpensive education for working-class children, some schools established a system of using student monitors. A teacher would supervise a number of older students, who would each run a class. One adult could then be indirectly in charge of several hundred children, greatly reducing costs. The system ultimately became quite popular in Great Britain and the United States (Graves 1971). In one variant the monitors distributed cash rewards to those children who excelled in their studies. Unfortunately, the system acquired a reputation for corruption, as some monitors learned to supplement their own salaries by, in effect, charging students a fee for good grades.

One might predict (at the risk of appearing naively optimistic) that, if pay-for-study were adopted in our junior and senior high schools today, we would have more success in curbing outright financial corruption. Yet a host of other problems would remain. Even without cash rewards teachers today often show favoritism. With the addition of cash rewards the ability to help a "deserving" family could add another dimension to the tendency toward favoritism. Moreover, we would still have the same measurement and distribution problems that arise when the schools endeavor to raise effort directly. If cash rewards go to the best performers, those who are more able than industrious are apt to obtain the higher rewards. And, since the more able generally come from families with higher socioeconomic status, payments by results would likely transfer resources to those who are better off.

Motivational researchers have also raised questions about the use of cash rewards. Some predict, on the basis of empirical work as well as theory, that the practice would have unintended, negative consequences. Mark Lepper and David Greene (1978, xi–xii) argue that, while extrinsic rewards can stimulate effort, they also have hidden costs, since the individual then focuses on aspects of performance directly relevant to the attainment of this reward. As a result, while paying rewards may have a positive influence on performance in certain respects, "it may also result in performance decrements along the dimensions not seen as relevant to the attainment of reward." Moreover, rewards "provide significant information about an individual's competence," which can have negative effects on the individual's self-esteem and, hence, on his or her performance. The authors find, too, that rewards "may also make issues of volition and compulsion salient to that person," with negative effects on performance.

According to the critics of reward systems, the negative effects become increasingly important as we move from more routine tasks (in which they only partially offset the positive effects of incentives) to more creative or difficult processes, such as learning new material (Condry and Chambers 1978; McGraw 1978). In these situations offering a reward may so reduce intrinsic motivation that achievement declines.[2] There is a continuing debate over these issues. Some psychologists disagree with the arguments of Lepper and Greene; some even maintain that cash rewards simply add to one's motivation to succeed (Skinner 1976).

Improved Information Flows between Students and Future Employers

A similarly negative prediction does not appear to attach to relating study effort to financial gain indirectly, by increasing both the certainty and the size of the relationship between earnings as an adult and study effort while in school. At the present time, however, such incentives are weakened by the limited amount and poor quality of information about students available to employers. We could correct this by making much better use of the information that is already being collected. Computers could collect and make available to employers a vast amount of information about the twelve or so years of a student's education, including grades, detailed course descriptions, any available scores on standardized achievement tests, honors won, extracurricular activities, letters of recommendation, and available data on absences, tardiness, or misbehavior in class. To protect privacy such information would be sent to the employer only at the request of the student. Some reformers suggest that plastic-protected transcripts be given to graduates, who could present them directly to potential employers, if they wished. If employers are permitted to obtain and use detailed information needed to place dropouts and graduates in jobs as they find appropriate, we can expect their interest in how well a job applicant did in school to increase sharply. Communication with employers can be further improved by honestly labeling courses, making it much easier for employers to evaluate the material they receive from schools.

There is, of course, resistance to such changes. Minority rights issues cannot be brushed aside. In the 1960s some employers used academic credentials inappropriately; standards were sometimes set to reduce the proportion of nonwhites in jobs in which these credentials were of little significance and, thus, to evade the newly enacted civil rights legislation. The legal remedy for this has been to require employers to prove that the credentials they use to screen applicants are related to on-the-job productivity, yet this can be a difficult case to make. Moreover, even if employers are convinced of its validity, they cannot be certain that the test will be accepted by a court. Nowadays, they often find it more prudent not to ask for credentials than to try to demonstrate to a federal bureaucrat or judge that, for example, an A grade in Latin III yields a better salesperson.

A related problem is that employers who do offer young people upward mobility within their organizations may want candidates for later promotion. The higher-level jobs often require more cognitive achievement than those at the entry level. Hence, there appears to be a conflict: if entry job requirements are set at the relatively high level that is in the best interest of the company, some applicants who are quite capable of doing entry-level work are turned down. This can lead to an increase in unemployment, given the relatively greater difficulty that poorly prepared youngsters have in finding any sort of suitable work. And a disproportionate amount of this burden will fall on minority youths.[3]

Perhaps the best hope for resolving these divisive issues lies in the realization that the present system imposes real hardships on minority youths. They are heavily represented in the "forgotten half" who enter the labor force without postsecondary schooling. The lack of useful information about their high school work in the hands of potential employers reduces both their incentives to study while in school and the probability that they will find decent employment upon graduation.[4]

National or Regional Examinations

National examination results on scholastic and other achievements can provide employers with a potentially useful supplement to the information now collected by schools in the United States (Finn 1991; National Center for Educational Statistics 1990). The extent to which this potential is realized will depend on whether current restrictions on the use of tests are lifted. If employers are encouraged to use academic data, then standardized national (or even statewide) examinations might make a significant contribution to increased study effort. We have seen that, in other countries, national examinations stimulate effort by students, teachers, and administrators.

Advocates of national examinations stress the importance of basing them on material learned in school, rather than the student's aptitude or abilities. Several examinations might be offered in the United States, including tests of manual skills and of the social skills needed to cooperate with others as well as of academic accomplishment. Academic examinations could be set at more than one level, so that, for example, youths who had already mastered calculus could take a more advanced mathematics test. A variety of tests would provide employers with a broad range of measurements. Students could choose to take some or all of the tests. Daniel and Lauren Resnick (1985) suggest some interesting ideas for tests designed to measure manual skills, those of a "project building" nature that might appeal to employers.

They also describe tests that can be performed with other students, to demonstrate one's ability both to learn and to work cooperatively, an important asset in the workplace (Commission on the Skills of the American Workforce 1990, 69).[5]

Those who oppose such tests argue that the exams might induce instructors to "teach to the test," that is, to prepare students for specific exams rather than teaching a broader range of materials.[6] Moreover, specialists argue that studying that is directed to a reward (in this case a student's doing well on an exam and thus being attractive to employers) will distort a student's learning effort. Advocates of this system of exams respond that the solution is to design tests that are sufficiently broad and deep to make it worthwhile for teachers and students to focus their efforts on them (Finn 1991, 263–66). They cite measures in other countries which meet these criteria. For example, examinations need not be of the multiple-choice type but, instead, can consist largely of essay questions that demand that the student reason systematically and express ideas clearly (and grammatically). To insure objectivity they can be graded anonymously, by personnel who are not in any way associated with the youngster's school.

Moreover, sociologists tell us that the present system of classroom exams, in which teachers are perceived as "marking on a curve," has negative effects on achievement, since students believe that they are competing with one another and, thus, are inclined toward group efforts to reduce studying. Replacing these tests with a more objective standard will improve performance (Covington 1984). Hence, national examinations may serve a positive motivational purpose.

Groups that oppose national examinations—for example, disadvantaged groups and residents of states with low academic standards—fear that members of their groups or areas will do poorly. Others have special views on the proper way to present a subject, or to measure achievement in it, and oppose any national standard that does not conform. There is disagreement over the teaching of even such a relatively noncontroversial subject as mathematics. In subjects such as history, literature, and other liberal arts, in which there is little agreement about what the course content should be, let alone its presentation, differences are sharper. To take just two examples, there is no consensus on the role that should be given to the political history of Asia or Africa relative to that of Europe. Or, again, there are those who want to give equal time to the history of literature in countries in which, until quite recently, people were illiterate.

Thus, a bruising battle lies ahead. Before giving up, however, we should recall the emphasis that our Japanese competitors (despite their alleged xenophobia) place on teaching *their* high school students the history and geography of Europe and North America and the history of Western thought.[7]

A Reformed System Can Demand More Effort

We know that the shabby treatment given to the three-quarters of American youths who do not finish college wastes important human talent. We stigmatize those who do not complete their schooling by labeling them dropouts.[8] Moreover, many students who do not actually drop out of school retreat from a college preparatory program to more or less meaningless curricula, obtaining a "general education" diploma that has very limited marketability. And neither the school nor the state provides much assistance in placing the graduate or the dropout when that person does enter the labor market. More attention to the career prospects of these young people, as in the German system, could have a positive effect on their morale and study effort.[9]

Proposed changes include linking schools and employers through much greater use of apprenticeships, work-study programs, and the like. Placement services that lead to the direct hiring of selected high school graduates for permanent jobs with upward mobility would also be helpful. These changes can directly improve the motivation of those who are not college bound: if students know there are training opportunities available, and that the better opportunities are reserved for those with good records, the so-called forgotten half has a strong incentive to work hard in school. The effort students do exert in school is also more efficiently directed when they have a clearer view of their career opportunities and can choose courses that will serve them after graduation.[10]

Adopting such programs in the United States will not be easy. There are the usual political difficulties: these programs require some additional government funding; a shift of educational resources among programs may be necessary, so that some bureaucracies lose resources, while others gain; and some educators and other administrators will need retraining.

Perhaps the most important impediment to change is the persistence of the so-called American dream: that young men and women can do anything they want to in life; even the dullest individual should not be told that becoming a first-class professional is most unlikely. These are strongly held beliefs. Sixty years ago the governor of Louisiana, Huey Long, captured the imagination of millions of Americans with the slogan Every Man a King, and this vision still has great power. Some critics will undoubtedly perceive reform programs as designed to restrict access to professional jobs, rather than as a way to upgrade millions from unskilled to highly skilled, well-paid, blue- or white-collar work.

We also know a process of selection which begins early in a person's life can impose psychological costs on anyone who receives a relatively low classification. Europeans have found that, despite a variety of governmental efforts to make lower classifications more acceptable to youngsters, low self-esteem remains a problem (Nothdurft 1989, 39). In the longer run, however, the net effect on self-esteem can be more positive. It is hard to see why, for example, at age eighteen or nineteen, the self-esteem of a young German apprentice or journeyman in a skilled, high-paying occupation should be lower than that of recent high school graduates in this country who find that they are unemployable unless they are willing to take the same type of service sector job they held on a part-time basis while students (Miller 1989).

Labor Market Reforms

Closer relations between schools and employers require changes in employment practices as well as reforms in education. The agenda recommended here makes the implicit assumption that U.S. employers will respond to a reformed education system by introducing new policies, such as offering good jobs to qualified young people, being willing to cooperate in work-study programs, and greatly increasing the number of apprenticeships.

But will this level of cooperation be forthcoming? While a reformed school system can be expected to attract some employers, we don't know that a *sufficient* number will change their practices to accommodate all those qualified youngsters interested in opportunities for training and upward mobility. Good opportunities are more likely to be offered in situations in which job tenure is longer: a company that expects youngsters to spend much of their working life with the same firm has a far greater incentive to make investments in their careers than one that expects new hires to leave soon. The greater willingness of European and Japanese companies to make large investments in young employees is often attributed to the long job tenures they expect. These long tenures are explained by tight labor markets and the steady economic growth that has enabled firms to keep workers employed as well as by government and union controls that make it extremely expensive to lay off a worker.[11]

Many responsible Americans believe that employers in this country should be induced to increase job tenures, yet it is not at all clear that this will happen. Documents such as the report of the Commission on the Skills of the American Workforce have been influential, but, nevertheless, one fears that a larger group of managers have on their night tables books that argue for shorter, not longer, job tenures. For example, in their recent study, *Workplace 2000*, Joseph Boyett and Henry Conn (1991) insist that, because we are entering an era of rapid technological change with fierce competition in the marketplace, few U.S. companies will be able to offer long-term, secure employment in the United States, and workers will have to expect a number of job moves. In other words, job tenure will decrease, not increase. The authors cite the need for much more on-the-job training and retraining as technology accelerates. This scenario raises a difficult question: In the absence of employer incentives, who will pay for on-the-job training in response to technological change?[12]

More School Choice

Schools now operate as part of a broad educational system, subject to democratic control at the community level. A restructuring of this system could raise achievement levels. Even without restructuring, national examinations combined with closer ties between schools and employers would give parents a much better idea of just how their schools serve, or fail to serve, students. If a significantly higher proportion of students in the next school district scored significantly better in knowledge-based exams and received significantly better jobs in local industry as a result, these parents would know about it and would likely complain to the school board about the weakness of their school. Faced with a public outcry, principals might find that blurring signals on achievement through Mickey Mouse courses was no longer a good strategy. When students with good grades in courses such as Twentieth-Century American Culture fail a national examination in basic English grammar, they may well fail to obtain decent employment, with negative consequences for the principals. Similarly, teachers will be somewhat less pressured to make classroom contracts that result in their students' failing to pass national examinations.

Nevertheless, raising effort within the present structure would still face obstacles. As long as schools must accept any student within their geographic area, delinquent youths would continue to sit in the same classrooms with hardworking students, and principals would still be pressed to find short-term solutions to try to please a variety of special interest groups as well as parents.

The most popular restructuring plans today call for some form of parental choice over the school their children attend. In one variant, put forward most eloquently by John Chubb and Terry Moe (1990), the government would continue to own and regulate the schools, but the schools would have to compete for students and funds the way private schools do today. Other proposals go further, allowing parents to use pay vouchers to enroll their children in private schools. Those favoring plans that increase parental choice say that it can have a positive effect on quality. To attract students, high schools would have to market their product to employers as well as colleges. They could, in principle, imitate the better private schools, which specialize in a high-quality product and provide clear signals to employers and colleges about the achievements of their students. This niche-marketing approach could be adopted most economically in the large metropolitan areas in which most Americans live.

Market pressures and a forceful principal can force complete reorganization within a school. Principals can be induced to cut costs or accelerate the learning process simply to survive. Competition provides an incentive to observe similar reforms elsewhere in the system and to adopt them, much like what is done in the private sector today.[13] They can also gain a competitive edge by applying efficient practices from industry and government to education. Innovative use of both standard business strategies and computer-based approaches to education could transform the system. Most important, when schools are rewarded for results, they have a reason to motivate their students. Hence, a restructuring of the system can be considered as a complementary strategy for stimulating student effort.

School choice plans, however, are very controversial.[14] Stakeholders in the present system, including unions of teachers and associations of school administrators, have opposed many of these plans, as have a number of academic investigators. Some minimize the predicted effects of choice, arguing that most children will continue to attend their neighborhood school (especially if the government is unwilling to provide free busing to their school of choice). Others insist that we have a social obligation to maintain schools that accept all children, including those who are physically, emotionally, and mentally handicapped, and also to "mainstream" these youngsters into classrooms with other children. Yet, if students can choose schools freely, the more capable among them may opt to associate with one another, thus defeating the goal of mainstreaming. Similarly, if, for example, either white or black students in a classroom prefer to associate only with those of their own race, efforts to integrate the class are frustrated.[15]

Another objection is that parents, especially those with little education themselves, are generally not in a good position to evaluate schools. Class differences in the ability to select schools can increase educational inequality and, very likely, the segregation of students according to their family's ethnic or socioeconomic background (Catterall 1992). Finally, some critics of school reorganization say that our public schools are rightly constrained to perform duties that serve broad social purposes, even at the expense of basic education. The hours of class time devoted to nonacademic activities in our public schools today are cited to indicate how important the community considers them.[16]

School choice plans that allow children to use their vouchers to pay tuition at private schools are still more controversial. While advocates believe that bringing in new types of schools will produce more meaningful competition and more rapid improvement in students' achievements, opponents predict that for-profit schools will enter the market, exploiting parental ignorance and failing to deliver even a minimally satisfactory product. Maintaining standards through government regulations will be much more difficult, critics argue, when a variety of private schools comes to dominate the market (Brown 1992).

Comparisons with other nations do not offer much help in resolving this controversy; while there is some room for choice within the school systems of other countries, it is typically less sweeping than that recommended by advocates of change in the United States. In fact, in many countries quality is maintained through strong central control: in some of them federal education ministries dictate the week's lesson plans for the nation's children.

This does not mean that a measure of school choice could not work here or that it should not be tried. After all, the United States is not Japan or Germany. If we are not willing to submit to a high level of central government control in the interest of having high-quality graduates, then we can explore alternatives that better fit our own traditions, such as a restructuring of our present state and local system which provides greater choice to individual families, perhaps with a larger role for the private sector.[17] The result could be further gains in student effort.

Complementary Policies

Clearly, raising effort requirements, improving the flow of information between students, employers, and schools, and restructuring schools to permit more parental choice complement one another in important ways. An increase in effort requirements without other reforms can yield an unacceptably high dropout rate. But this negative impact can be blunted if increased requirements are accompanied by better information flows. If achievement tests are offered to all students, who can then choose whether to pass the results on to employers, and if employers use the information they receive to select and assign employees, students have a stronger incentive to work harder. If better information about graduates induces employers to offer jobs with opportunities for training and possible upward mobility to youngsters upon graduation, rather than dead-end jobs, students will be similarly motivated to work harder at school. If the student body is interested in learning, school administrators can reform curricula and encourage teachers to assign more homework without increasing the dropout rate.

If vouchers are introduced under present circumstances some families will choose the wrong school because they lack good information: a school that invests money in a new building or in a successful athletic program might attract some students who are not even aware of its academic strengths or shortcomings. Yet, if choice is combined with a sharp improvement in the information flow from the labor market to students, and from students to employers, one important objection to school choice is answered. Parents can more easily learn what their child's chances are of doing well at a given school before committing to that school; later, in the labor market, employers can determine how well suited he or she is for a particular job.

Many advocates of school choice believe that achievement tests and other measures meant to improve communication can only yield full benefits if they are accompanied by some form of school choice. Choice, the argument goes, forces schools to respond to the new information provided about student success, with the result that more effective courses of study will be offered. Combining the strategies of higher requirements, better information, and school choice should produce still further gains.[18] For example, in cases in which employers and students are well informed and families choose the schools their children will attend, students' willingness to supply effort should be enhanced. In a best-case scenario this combination of reforms creates an environment favorable to school system–wide initiatives to increase student effort, such as lengthening the school day or year, which are not politically acceptable at present.

Conclusion

Is Basic Reform Likely?

The forces arrayed against basic change in our educational system range from organized interest groups[1] to a strong feeling by U.S. citizens that present practices reflect a traditional American approach that should not be abandoned lightly. Attempts to extract more effort through changes in the system have encountered organized opposition, conservative resistance to departure from tradition, and just plain indifference and inertia.

Pressure to change builds when no comfortable alternative seems available, as was the case when the New Deal was enacted in the 1930s, economic controls were imposed during World War II, and math and science education was revamped and reemphasized following the Soviet launch of Sputnik. Many Americans these days feel that we have somehow "lost it," that only radical institutional reform will maintain our country's place as a leader among nations as well as U.S. living standards. This anxiety focuses on the poor performance of our educational system.

The clamor for reform heard after *A Nation at Risk* first appeared has not died down, and, though both the Bush and Clinton administrations have agreed that change is needed, it is still not clear whether basic reforms will be undertaken. Major changes were not made under President Bush. The Clinton administration advocates some important legislative initiatives that support change, yet it is far from clear how it will deal with the tough questions posed in this book. For example, with federal assistance we are now developing standards for most of the subjects taught in the K–12 system (the last will be ready by 1997).[2] The government asserts that the new standards will be "world class" and that all American youths will meet them. Setting such standards is a step in the right direction, but we still do not know whether they will be applied by every state to every student, whether examinations will determine how well students meet these standards, whether the exam results will be passed on to potential employers in a form useful in making hiring decisions, or whether employers will be permitted to use them freely.

There are a number of other problems. The groups responsible for establishing standards for the different disciplines are not well coordinated: for example, preliminary reports suggest that, while in some subject areas standards will be spelled out in great (perhaps excessive) detail, in others there will only be broad guidelines. Interest groups representing those with limited English proficiency or those who are slow learners argue that the national standards are not appropriate for their clients. Teachers disagree strongly about how best to help students meet higher standards. Some legislators insist that a new system of federal standards be postponed until the schools have met the so-called opportunity to learn criteria—that is, that every student, whether in an inner city, rural slum, or affluent suburb, will have equal access to school-based resources, including qualified teachers, reasonably small classes, good computer, laboratory, and library facilities, and music, art, and physical education programs, as well as a safe school environment with clean, well-maintained buildings. Some well-known figures in the reform movement are now openly skeptical about the prospects for meaningful standards.[3]

Examinations on these standards are still in the development stage, and a number of questions must be resolved here as well. For example, if legislators insist on a "one test fits all" principle, the resulting examination will either fail to discriminate among our more advanced students or will be so rigorous as to produce an unacceptably high standard for those whose skills are below average.

Finally, it is not yet clear how efforts to avoid discrimination against women and nonwhites will affect the development and implementation of standards, curricula, and examinations.[4]

The Clinton administration has also proposed initiatives for improving the transition from school to work by building a national network of skills boards to set standards for a number of broad occupational groupings. These standards would then be used to guide high school students, as well as students in postsecondary training institutes, who would pick a career major organized around particular occupational groupings, such as health and biomedical sciences. Here, too, there are unsettled issues. Tensions between meritocratic and egalitarian goals raise troubling questions (e.g., how many high school seniors who hope to become surgeons will take the same courses as those who expect to process claims for Blue Cross?). Another difficulty is cited by employer groups; they ask how proposed federal skills boards, on which the business community has fewer than one-third of the seats, can generate standards that employers will accept. Introduction of the system might also be delayed because skills standards, like academic standards, will have to meet equal opportunity requirements: all students in a state must have the necessary school-based resources before the federal government will certify the state's skills standards.[5]

Some of these conflicts will likely be resolved through the political process. Others reflect long-held positions of well-organized interest groups, are not so easily resolved, and will continue to plague the reform effort. Nevertheless, the persistent, even growing, demand for reform is a positive sign.

Basic reform of the educational and labor market systems could have a dramatic impact. There is no good reason why student effort cannot be increased to, say, European levels. The result could well be sharp improvements in student effort and achievement, even among disadvantaged youngsters. We have a great untapped resource: the leisure of the American student. If an incentive system can unleash this power, substantial and dramatic progress is likely. We might not outstrip the best of our European or Asian competitors, but we could narrow the gap between us. There are ways to get our kids to study. What it takes is the determination to change.

Notes

Introduction

1. The analysis of the determination of labor supply requires an understanding of the rewards to labor as well as of the motivation of the person supplying effort.

Chapter 1: Our Kids Don't Study Much

1. See Karweit 1983; Sedlak and others 1986; and Bachman, Johnston, and O'Malley 1984.

2. See note 7 below.

3. "Total spending by all levels of government is expected to increase by five per cent to a total of $445 billion [this year]." It has increased by 40 percent, adjusted for inflation, in the past ten years (*Education Week*, 2 September 1992). At the long-term rate, inflation-adjusted expenditures would equal half a trillion dollars in three and a half years. If the annual 5 percent increase in unadjusted dollars continues, dollar outlays would reach this level in less than two and a half years.

4. See Barber 1986; Epstein 1988; Frederick and Walberg 1980; Holsinger 1982; Johnson 1978; Karweit 1983; Keith 1982; Keith and others 1986; National Assessment of Educational Progress 1986a; Natriello and McDill 1986; Paschal, Weinstein, and Walberg 1984; Schmidt 1983; Shanahan and Walberg 1985; Stallings 1980; Walberg, Paschal, and Weinstein 1986.

5. I argue in chapter 6 that one result of irrelevant teaching is to further reduce student effort.

6. See Grant Foundation 1988, 130; Kearns and Doyle 1988; National Center on Education and the Economy 1990, 23; Nothdurft 1989, 3. The rising proportion of young Americans enrolled in colleges and other postsecondary institutions provides a (very expensive) way to help offset the efforts of leisurely study habits at earlier ages.

7. Also see Camber and Keeves 1973; Husen 1967, 1982; Inkeles 1979; International Assessment for the Evaluation of Education Achievement 1988; Stevenson 1986. A National Assessment of Educational Progress study found that when U.S. youngsters were asked, "How much time did you spend on homework yesterday?" 37 percent of the fourth-graders, 26 percent of eighth-graders, and 33 percent of eleventh-graders said none. Only 20 percent of the

fourth-graders, 38 percent of eighth-graders, and 41 percent of eleventh-graders said that they did an hour or more of homework. Note that these data are based on statements by the students themselves, not on objective observations (Anderson, Mead, and Sullivan 1986a). In another national study only 29 percent of upper-level high school students (those who had been sophomores two years earlier) spent at least five hours per week on homework (National Center for Educational Statistics 1984).

8. Of course, if we take a very long-term view and compare conditions in our schools today with public schools in mid-nineteenth-century U.S. cities, a more positive assessment of change might be made. For example, David Tyack (1974, 38) reports that in the Chicago school system in 1850 there were 13,500 school-age children, of whom 1,919 were actually in school; they were taught by 21 teachers. By 1860 enrollment had increased to 14,000 and the number of teachers to 123. Seats were scarce, and low achievers were simply expelled.

9. See Kurth 1988; Rock and others 1985; and Rothman 1990. For declines in scores, see Bishop 1989c; and Murray and Herrnstein 1992. See Bishop 1989b for a recent attempt to ascertain the effects of declines in scores on productivity.

10. The SAT is not an achievement test per se, but it does reflect achievement as well as aptitude and has the advantage that average scores are available over a relatively long period of time.

11. The disparity in mathematics achievement dropped from four years to less than three in the same period (Bishop 1991, 529).

Chapter 2: Students Prefer To Do Other Things

1. Csikszentmihalyi and Larson 1984, 39: "Its faculty was highly professional . . . many of the classes we visited were masterpieces of teaching artistry."

2. According to some economists, the effect of consumer advertising campaigns by firms is largely to induce customers to switch from one brand to another, rather than to change their underlying preferences.

3. Gintis's theory does have a number of indirect implications. As Marxists, Gintis and his colleague Samuel Bowles later developed and refined a thesis that our educational system is well suited for training young people for their future class roles, predicting that children of factory workers are socialized to get to work on time, to take orders, and to believe that their intellectual powers are no greater than their routine jobs demand, while children of managers and professional people are socialized to innovate, to make decisions, and to lead others. It is true that curricula and school climate do vary with the socioeconomic status of the local district. (Compare this thesis with the discussion in Carnoy and Levin 1985.) Most observers, however, would question whether the U.S. educational system is meeting the needs of the "capitalists." If the level of cognitive achievement of our young people is adequate preparation for

the industrial system of, say, the early twentieth century, the needs of the economic order cannot be said to be met. (This argument is developed further in chap. 10.) Also see Katz 1971, for a discussion of the influence of class in U.S. education in earlier times.

4. A useful survey of this literature is found in Ames and Ames 1984, 1985, and 1989. For a more critical view, see Smelser 1989.

5. "For young children, high ability is implied by learning or by success at tasks that they are uncertain of being able to complete. They do not judge ability with reference to performance norms or social comparison" (Nicholls 1984, 47). Also see Weiner 1984.

6. See Covington 1984; Nicholls 1984; and Stipek 1984.

7. This argument implies a deferred psychic return to study effort in the early years of school. If students work hard when they begin schooling, they will arrive at the upper grades with a higher skill level. Students will then be more likely to be able to follow the teacher's presentation of the advanced material in the upper grades as well as the new textbook. The time cost of mastering a new increment of knowledge is reduced as a result. Moreover, they are likely to receive better grades and other signs of approval from the teacher. All this will protect their self-esteem, make study less unpleasant, and hence, if we accept the view of these psychologists, encourage them to work harder. (I owe this point to an anonymous referee.)

8. Csikszentmihalyi and Larson (1984, 260) are guardedly optimistic. "It is very difficult for teachers to make academic learning enjoyable when young people lack even the simplest intellectual skills. Difficult, but not impossible. If paraplegics can learn to enjoy playing basketball, a TV-reared generation can surely learn to enjoy the use of the mind."

9. The current status given in those media to serious students may tell us more about the true American attitude toward intellectual endeavors than do the pious pronouncements of politicians, college presidents, and serious newspaper columnists. (See the discussion of national attitudes below.)

10. Cynics have pointed out, however, that the falloff in the study effort of Japanese students who have passed their examinations and gained admission to university (thus assuring them of a good job upon graduation) belies the view that these youngsters really prize learning for its own sake.

11. This treatment of ability differences in Japan may also help to protect the child's self-esteem and so promote a more positive attitude toward further learning.

12. But see note 3 in chapter 8 for an indication of recent changes in French attitudes. See also White 1987, 18, for a discussion of the Japanese system of daily, rigorous physical exercise in school.

13. The negative portrayal of serious students in so much of the popular media provides another obvious example.

14. This debate brings out other issues that are also relevant to the discus-

sion of policies to increase student effort. Critics point out that a longer school year or day will require more taxes, while supporters cite the useful babysitting function it will provide for working parents.

15. These attitudes have very deep roots in the past. In primitive societies adults not only socialize youths to the value of the group but also instruct them in its religion, traditions, and the (mythological) history of the tribe and of the world around them. Typically, intensive and prolonged initiation rites will include learning a considerable amount of oral material (Campbell 1959). Only through undergoing these rites of passage does the individual become an acceptable adult member of the tribe. Modern societies are more complex, but educational systems are assigned at least some of the responsibilities of "initiating" the young.

16. Obviously, youngsters (as in all societies) are socialized to the less formal aspects of their culture.

17. This statement is subject to one qualification: the last chapters recommend policies to increase the relevance of study effort to future career success. If students perceive their studies as having a more direct connection to future rewards, their attitudes toward studying will likely improve.

18. Csikszentmihalyi and Larson (1984) collected empirical evidence of these preferences in the same study that found that students held negative attitudes toward homework and time spent in the classroom.

19. Japanese high school students also spend more time watching television than do students in many other countries. They spend much less time, however, socializing with friends. As a result, they spend virtually as many hours doing homework as they do watching television (Rohlen 1983, 275).

20. See the discussion of this paradox in chapter 3.

21. Bachman and others 1978; Greenberger and Steinberg 1986, 18–21; Lewin-Epstein 1981; National Assessment of Educational Progress 1986b; Yang, Lester, and Gatto 1989.

22. Research also indicates that part-time work does not have the positive effects on a teenager's development that many parents hope for: more often, it engenders negative attitudes toward work relationships (Greenberger and Steinberg 1986, 132–34). For example, almost one-half of high school students who are employed part-time admit to some form of dishonest behavior on the job. Drinking, smoking, and gambling are also more common among those students who are employed part-time.

23. Sedlak reports that school administrators generally are favorably disposed toward student part-time employment in local businesses, partly because they believe it improves students' relationships with the community.

24. For example, we can question whether the fact that Japanese adolescents spend much less time than U.S. adolescents socializing with their friends explains their increased hours of study.

Chapter 3: Why Study?

1. Other extrinsic benefits include his or her improved performance as a consumer (see Michael 1973).

2. For example, if an 8 percent reduction in hours yielded a similar drop in output directly, addition of the schooling effect might increase the long-term total cost to 15 to 16 percent of output (see the calculations in Owen 1989).

3. Even then the relationship is problematical. Young people as well as adults did put in long hours of work in the nineteenth century, but most American children were on farms, where study time had to compete with chore time. (See the discussion below of long-term trends in student part-time employment.)

4. There were some commonalities. Part of the apparent decline in student effort is attributed to a reduction in student attention in class. Stafford and Duncan (1985) report a similar decline in on-the-job effort in the adult labor force in the same period.

5. There are exceptions. See Becker 1981 for a discussion of the argument that increased governmental support for young people will undermine parental control over them.

6. More generally, one can model two-generational family decision making in which the income and leisure preferences of both parents and child, over the lifetimes of both, are considered in determining the study effort of the latter as well as the work effort of the former. One can then assume either that this information is used to maximize the welfare of the family as a whole or that there is conflict concerning outcomes.

7. Economists theorizing about the employer-employee relationship today rely heavily on analyses of the "principal agent" problem, in which an individual or group appoints another as its agent to carry out its will but lacks the ability to obtain full compliance. Examples include stockholders and managers, union members and union officers, and employers and employees.

8. Employers will also endeavor to socialize workers to the norms of the company, for much the same reason.

9. See West 1992 for historical background on these differences. It is worth noting that for hundreds of years the guild symbol for schoolteachers in England was a cane.

10. Unless parents come to realize that the long-term cost to the family of students' shirking has increased, pari passu, with the rising opportunity cost of adult time. Then even well-paid adults may see that the interest of the family is better served if more time is spent insuring that the study effort of their children is maintained.

11. Of course, hard work by young employees may also have a deferred payoff, as when it puts them on a "fast track" to promotion.

12. They do, however, receive *nonfinancial* rewards right away in the form of high grades, informal praise, or public awards. (See the discussion in chap. 6.)

13. For this reason one might expect less intrafamily conflict over the length of the workday during the period when child labor was common (at least, when children were allowed to profit from the fruits of their labor).

14. This model is modified when scheduling influences profitability in other ways. For example, fixed costs per employee (such as training costs or medical costs) encourage longer schedules, while the effect of fatigue on the quality of work discourages them (see Owen 1979).

15. Alternatively, if less plausibly, employers could operate schools, teaching subjects that would maximize the value of the graduate to the firm and insuring youngsters an appropriate reward for their effort. Employer-operated schools would have a number of obvious disadvantages that would, in the author's opinion, more than offset this single gain.

16. These influences will be discussed further in chapter 6.

17. Exclusion of part-timers from the fringe benefits paid to full-timers, such as health care, which were rising rapidly in this period, very likely has also contributed to the growing demand for those working less than full-time.

18. The inner-city youth's net wage per hour of effort from working in the suburbs is low because of time and money spent in commuting. This disadvantage is compounded insofar as he or she lacks information on job opportunities and faces employment discrimination in the suburbs.

19. This is, of course, a consequence of our having comparatively recently achieved the status of "affluent society." (See the discussion in chap. 2 of the use of youth earnings in past generations.)

20. Poor education will also limit his or her ability to use time and income effectively to create pleasurable experiences. (But see chap. 6 for a more skeptical argument.)

Chapter 4: Does Studying Pay? Returns to Those Staying in School

1. Some writers on human capital theory tend to emphasize cognitive achievement to the exclusion of socialization. But both factors can enhance the value of the employee to the firm.

2. See, for example, Blaug 1985; Layard and Psacharopoulos 1974; Rohling 1986; Spence 1974; Stiglitz 1975; and Wolpin 1977.

3. Sedlak goes on to argue that since the 1950s and 1960s the role of the high school has changed once again, as attendance has become quasi-universal; the diploma no longer signals above-average ability. There is a stigma if you "drop out" which does hurt your prospects in the job market (Sedlak and others 1986).

Other critics of U.S. education would disagree with Sedlak in certain respects, arguing that the economy has changed as the school system changed, so that now much more cognitive achievement as well as proper socialization is needed.

4. Moreover, our unwillingness to stream teenagers into narrow occupational training means that much of what they learn which would be of interest to some employers may not be of interest to the employers who hire them.

5. Compare the earnings obtained by those at higher and lower levels of schooling (say, those with one year of college and high school graduates) over the lifetimes of individuals. Compare these earnings increments (the returns to education) to their costs (the earnings lost from staying in school an extra year, plus the tuition, books, and other direct costs). The rate of return equates the discounted value of future returns to current costs. It is typically measured as being around 6 to 8 percent in real terms (even after being adjusted for ability and socioeconomic background).

6. There is a vast literature on this payoff. See, for example, Barton 1989; Beaton 1974; Becker 1975; Blackburn and others 1990; Blaug 1985; Boissiere, Knight, and Sabot 1985; Bryan 1988; Card and Krueger 1990; Chiswick 1988; Freeman 1975; Heckman and Polachek 1974; Hirschorn 1988; Jencks and others 1972, 1979; Katz and Murphy 1992; Kodde 1986, 1988; Kolstad 1982; Lazear 1977a, 1977b; Manski 1989; Mincer 1984; Rumberger 1981, 1983; Tsang 1987; Tsang and Levin 1985; Verdugo and Verdugo 1989; and Wachtel 1974.

7. "Skill requirements of the new jobs being created in our economy are increasing" (Nothdurft 1989, 3).

8. Clune 1989; Firestone, Fuhrman, and Kirst 1989. Toch (1991) notes that in many states and localities participation in athletics and other extracurricular activities has been made dependent on satisfactory grades; that pep rallies, field trips, and other nonacademic activities during the school day have been banned; and that there have been increases in classes per day and school days per year. Scholarships based on merit rather than need have been offered in some localities, and there has been a near-doubling of high school students taking examinations for advanced placement.

Chapter 5: The Return to Those Who Leave School

1. While direct evidence of the influence of study effort is scarce, there have been numerous efforts to measure the effect on earnings of ability or achievement scores (holding years of schooling constant). These effects are typically found to be relatively small, though often statistically significant. See, for example, Beaton 1974; Behrman and others 1980; Bishop 1987, 1989c; Boissiere, Knight, and Sabot 1985; Bound, Griliches, and Hall 1986; Eberts and Stone 1988; Griliches and Mason 1972; Hause 1972, 1974; Hauser and Daymont 1977; Lazear 1977a, 1977b; Olnek and Taubman 1977; Taubman and Wales 1974; Willis and Rosen 1979; and Wise 1975a, 1979. If schools that are "higher quality" elicit more study effort from pupils, then evidence of the effect of quality on later success is relevant. See, for example, Behrman and Birdsall

1983; Card and Krueger 1990; Hanushek 1986; Summers and Wolfe 1977; and Welch 1973.

2. Bishop (1990) describes a six-year study of a panel of youths, fifteen to twenty-two years of age at the beginning of the study. He reports findings based on earnings in the last years of the study period. This panel was not restricted to high school graduates. Dropouts and those with college or other further education were included. Achievement effects were estimated, however, in a multivariate analysis in which years of schooling was also included as an independent variable.

3. The differences are quite large: an 11 percent improvement from a one standard deviation increase in Auto and Shop Information score against a 3 percent decrease from a similar increase in the verbal score. See also Bishop 1987, 1989c, and 1992.

4. This relatively high estimate in part reflects Bishop's innovative methodology (which, he claims, corrects for measurement error in past studies). His exclusion of young adults from his sample may also help to account for the more positive findings.

5. Yet another source of bias is introduced insofar as those individuals who are more able expend more study effort while in school.

6. The author also cites the fear of Equal Employment Opportunity Commission challenges to such questions. See Jones and Jackson (1990) for a positive view of the effects of college grades on the earnings of a group of business graduates.

7. Survey based on members of the NFIB (Bishop 1990, 114).

8. See Ascher 1988; Chamberlain and Griliches 1977; Cohany 1986; Fetters 1975; Fetters, Brown, and Owings 1984; Grant Foundation 1988; Holsinger 1982; Kramer 1989; Lewis 1988; Meyer and Wise 1982; Miller 1989; Nolfi 1978; Orazem and Mattila 1986; Sewell and Hauser 1975; Weiss 1988; Wise 1975, 1979; and Wise and Meyer 1984.

9. According to one American human resources expert: "In the U.S., the top employers ignore recent high school graduates and consider only applicants with extensive work experience. . . . The entire graduating class appears to employers as one undifferentiated mass of unskilled and undisciplined workers" (Bishop 1989a, 32).

10. See Barron, Black, and Loewenstein 1989; Garen 1988; Hersch and Reagan 1990; Liu 1986; Lockwood 1986; McCall 1990; and Mortensen 1988. Also see the discussion in chapter 4.

11. It was noted above that economic theory predicts that those with ability and/or good work ethics make investments in themselves by taking positions that (though they may pay less initially or afford less leisure time) will provide advancement for those who are able and hardworking. If these individuals are also those who worked hard in school, they will likely be found among the more successful in later life.

Of course, some good students will find that their later performance in employment situations does not live up to the expectations based on their work in school; some good students lack other qualities that are useful to an employer (such as interpersonal skills).

12. This constraint does not apply to subjects (such as typing) which a student might find immediately useful upon graduation.

Chapter 6: Limiting Incentives at School

1. Useful discussions of the social conditions in our schools are found in Boyer 1983; Cusick 1983; DiPrete and others 1987; Goodlad 1984; Morris and others 1984; Powell, Farrar, and Cohen 1985; Sedlak and others 1986; Sizer 1984; and Wirt and Kirst 1982. The National Association of Secondary School Principals (1985) carried out an empirical study of ninth-grade pupils that came to sharply different conclusions: students, teachers, and administrators were found to be good to excellent.

2. See also Bidwell 1965; Carroll 1963; Meyer, Scott, and Strang 1987; Weick 1976; and Williamson 1975, 1980. For useful micro-level theories of classrooms, see Brown and Saks 1975, 1980, 1981, 1987; and Mulligan 1984. For useful discussion of empirical studies of the effects of classroom organization on students, see, for example, Cohen 1983; Farrar 1983; McPartland and McDill 1977; Myers and others 1987; Neufeld and others 1983; Peng and others 1982; Purkey and Smith 1983; Rutter 1983; and Rutter and others 1979.

3. See LeCompte and Dworkin 1991 for an interesting analysis of teachers who "burn out" at an early age yet continue to teach for many years because they cannot find equal remuneration in other lines of work. The authors' empirical analysis of the ways in which misguided reform efforts have exacerbated the burnout problem in the 1980s is especially interesting to those seeking positive change.

4. On unionism, see Cohen and Murnane 1985; Kurth 1987; and Lieberman 1980, 1989.

5. Toch (1991) presents an interesting analysis of efforts by reformers in the 1980s to improve incentives for teachers—by establishing career ladders, introducing merit pay, permitting principals to select incoming teachers on some basis other than seniority, and the like. He also describes the success of organized efforts by teachers to block, or at least water down, many such initiatives.

6. Teachers are also reasonably well satisfied by this arrangement. While the majority find it easy to go along with the "contract," the minority that insists on rigor can be matched with students who want rigor, in the high-ability track (Powell, Farrar, and Cohen 1985).

7. See also the discussion in Hanson 1979.

8. In the heated debate that continues on this issue Chubb and Moe have been attacked as offering an idealized picture of private schools, characterizing

the system in terms of its independent schools, although the majority are actually affiliated with the Catholic church and other religious institutions.

9. Callahan (1962), Cremin (1962), Cubberley (1920), Ravitch (1974, 1983), and Tyack (1974) offer useful historical explanations of how certain features of our school system developed.

10. In an egalitarian society with mass communication, they ask, is an individual who enjoys a first-rate production of Shakespeare or can read the works Racine or Goethe in the original, or of Ovid or Aeschylus, really happier than someone who prefers to sit down in front of a large-screen TV on Sunday with a six-pack of beer to watch football? Might he not feel better at work on Monday, joining in the common discussion of the game?

11. Eric Hanushek (1992) argues that a lack of knowledge about the relation between school inputs and educational outcomes increases resistance to change.

12. The empirical work of Richard Miguel and Robert Faulk (1984) reveals perceptions of future employment opportunities among high school students. Students generally had a good understanding of the positive behavior needed to get a job and to succeed but had a poor understanding of how important it was to avoid bad behavior. Bad behavior included providing false information on an employment application, having a past conviction for marijuana use, being late for a job interview, being confused when asked a simple question during an interview, asking for significantly more than the job normally pays, not being able to read a newspaper, using bad grammar, having a poor school attendance record, or having dropped out of school.

Chapter 7: Should We Care? The Role of Social Policy

1. See Thurow 1975.

2. One can think of the social benefits of education as a public good, whose consumption is shared by a large number of people. They cannot be excluded from the benefit and so cannot be counted on to pay for it as individuals. At the same time, their "consumption" of the benefit does not reduce the consumption of others. For example, if it is conceded that education enhances political decision making, then (1) other citizens benefit regardless of whether they pay for education, and (2) their consumption of the benefit does not reduce the benefit to other citizens. These conditions are the standard for a "public good" in the literature.

3. See the discussion of these criteria in Musgrave 1984.

4. See Haveman and Wolfe 1984; Levin 1972; Owen 1975; Weisbrod 1964.

5. This statement does not imply that we can simply compare the earnings of high school and college graduates to obtain the effect of college on earnings or productivity. That method would exaggerate the contribution of education, insofar as colleges select a group that is above average in ability (see Denison 1962).

6. The crude argument is that (abstracting from any effects of labor supply

on the proportion of output obtained by capital as profit and interest) an increase in output so obtained will yield an equal percentage increase in the income of capital.

7. Some such understanding presumably underlies the support of business lobbyists for increased immigration and increased female labor force participation and their opposition to reduced hours of work.

8. The long-term decline in the adult male workweek has been discussed by economists for generations. Economic theory predicts that this decline has had negative externalities: lower profits for business and smaller tax revenues for government (see Owen 1989).

9. See also Jablonski, Rosenblum, and Kinze 1988; Jorgenson 1987; U.S. Congress 1990; and Warswick 1985.

10. These feelings are real, whether they result from an actual decline in living standards or simply from a slower rate of growth.

11. There is some indirect statistical evidence for this in the findings that capital in this country tends to be a complement with skilled labor rather than unskilled labor.

12. Business also has a taxpayer interest in reducing the cost of schooling, and this has sometimes led to fewer resources for education. For a historical review of business opposition to federal aid to education, see Buis 1953. See also the discussion in Owen 1975.

13. If achievement in school seriously misled employers about productivity, a negative social effect could result. For example, requiring high test scores for applicants may rule out competent members of a minority group. But if employers know that the scores of applicants from this group systematically underestimate their ability to perform on the job, the employers have an incentive to correct for this bias. Only if they fail to do so will there be a negative social effect.

14. This calculation yields a rate of return which can be compared to the rate of return with returns from similar investments in physical capital.

15. Even if one accepts the social benefits of increased student effort and rejects the validity of unfettered student choice, one could still ask whether the present system adequately reflects the goal of obtaining a satisfactory level of effort. In theory our educational institutions could elicit a level of effort greater than the social optimum. The description of our schools given in chapter 6, however, gives scant support to this theoretical possibility.

16. Reasons for hesitating to propose government regulation of a private market include not only purely political difficulties but also more valid objections. For example, regulation is costly; in complex decision making the regulators often have less information at their disposal than does the private management they oversee; and regulation is frequently subject to bureaucratic and political biases. Moreover, regulatory decisions must be made in the presence of great uncertainty about expected benefits and costs.

17. Obvious exceptions would occur if a reform recommended either adding another layer of regulation or moving to a somewhat less regulated system.

18. As long as moving even a small amount of subsidy from duration of schooling to effort while in school will yield an increase in achievement (see the discussion in chap. 9).

Chapter 8: Borrowing from Abroad

1. Moreover, we know that considerable factual knowledge is necessary if one is to function as a "culturally literate" person in our society (see Hirsch 1987; Ravitch and Finn 1987).

2. The narrowness of education in Japan is exaggerated in accounts in our popular media, giving the public a misleading impression. For example, how many know that every Japanese child must learn to play two musical instruments, one wind and one keyboard, by the end of sixth grade? (Rohlen 1983, 116).

3. Of course, attitudes are changing in other countries. Many of King's examples of positive student attitudes are taken from France, but the *Economist* of 23 November 1991 reports that "a recent American film *The Dead Poets Society* became something of a cult in Paris. It is about a teacher who rebels against hidebound practices in an American school. This improbable export struck a chord with the French." Our press also reports demands for change in the Japanese school system.

4. Structural changes in the U.S. family may be making it more difficult to provide this support. Factors often cited here include the large number of children raised in poverty and the declining proportion raised in two-parent homes. Some see the declining numbers in single-earner, two-parent homes as an additional limitation. But Reginald Clark's (1983) in-depth study of ten low-income black households found that family culture variables—such as whether parents carefully monitored study effort, gave strong support to this effort, and disciplined children only in the latter's interest—were crucial in determining the academic success of their children, not family structure variables as such.

5. See also Rosenbaum and Kariya 1989, for a discussion of Japanese practice.

6. By reducing the loss associated with "termination" from more stringent programs, it also reduces the opposition to more selectivity in higher education. (See the discussion of these problems in chaps. 9 and 10.)

Chapter 9: Can Our Schools Demand More Effort?

1. See Levin and Tsang 1987; Link and Mulligan 1986; National Education Association 1987; Pace 1983.

2. Alexander, Cook, and McDill 1978; Alexander and Pallas 1984; Gamoran 1987; Lee and Bryk 1988. Some regard "mastery learning" as a benign substitute for tracking. Students can be assigned a learning task and be allowed

enough time to master it thoroughly before moving on to the next, more demanding task. Advocates can argue that this is less likely to be harmful to the slow learner than the traditional system, which forces the student to move on before he or she understands the current assignment and, thus, not only diminishes his or her self-confidence and self-esteem but leaves the student without the tools he or she needs to understand the next assignment.

3. See Ekstrom and others 1986; LeCompte and Dworkin 1991; Natriello 1987; Wehlage and Rutter 1986. Also see Kearns and Doyle 1988; U.S. Department of Education 1991.

4. The mathematical properties are developed in a paper, "Optimal Termination Rates for Students," available on request from the author.

5. The empirical evidence indicates that the average high school student picks easier courses when core curriculum requirements are relaxed (Sedlak and others 1986, 43).

6. This assumption need not hold under all conditions. In 1909 Helen Todd interviewed children working in what we would call sweatshops. She asked them, "If your father had a good job and you didn't have to work, which would you rather do—go to school or work in a factory?" Of the 500 respondents 412 said they preferred the factory. The reason given for this choice by 261 of the children was: "They don't hit you there" (Todd 1913). Ekstrom and colleagues (1986) present evidence on the similar attitudes of high school dropouts in the 1980s.

7. The effects on student reaction functions of other subsidy policies, including those associated with the development of our welfare state, are more difficult to predict. Welfare state policies may undermine the incentive to work hard, either in school or in the workplace. At the same time, however, if Aid to Families with Dependent Children (AFDC) assistance ceases when a teenager leaves school, the family is given a financial incentive to require the child to meet the school's requirements for remaining in school.

For further discussion of the economics of effort, see, for example, Becker 1985; Bowles 1977; Lazear 1981; and Shapiro and Stiglitz 1984.

8. To obtain the present value of wealth, future gains and costs are discounted back to the present by an appropriate rate of interest.

9. Of course, taxpayers are not monolithic; some are parents or employers and, hence, have diverse interests in educational outlays. Only insofar as they act in terms of their interest as taxpayers would the text analysis apply.

10. This will give taxpayers a special interest in school completion by lower-class students, if they expect these youngsters to be more likely than others to apply for welfare if they fail to finish school.

11. This is achieved today, albeit crudely, in our system of decentralized school systems. One large metropolitan area will contain many school districts. The system permits the use of different standards in different districts. Those with mostly disadvantaged students can set achievement standards that are

lower than average while maintaining *effort* standards that may be comparable to those from more favored districts.

12. But if students are not tracked by ability and industry, and requirements are lowered sufficiently to accommodate the lazy and less capable, the more ambitious students will be dissatisfied with the slow pace of instruction: some will become bored and actually leave; others will stay, but their work ethic will likely be damaged.

There are psychologists who raise yet another objection to increasing effort requirements or achievement standards, emphasizing the negative effects on those who do not do well. In a 1987 report, for example, the National Education Association uses psychological evidence to argue that letting students know where they stand relative to the national average will, for many students, especially those who are average or below average, have negative effects on happiness and self-esteem. Their motivation may be reduced, and the overall effect, on balance, could be that they put less effort toward study.

13. Sedlak and his colleagues (1986, 5) forecast opposition to higher standards from students, including more violent, disruptive behavior.

14. According to Firestone, Fuhrman, and Kirst 1989, this improvement was typically found in the weakest schools in the state, in which requirements had departed furthest from the newly emerging social norm.

15. A company differs from a school in that standards are set in terms of profit and loss rather than social benefits and costs, but this does not materially alter the analysis in the text.

16. See Nothdurft's 1989 study for the Brookings Institution for a useful discussion of these apprenticeship systems. See Hamilton 1990 for an in-depth comparison of the German and U.S. systems for managing the transition from school to work.

17. In some states a third choice, the Realschule, is offered (ibid.).

18. But see Hamilton 1990 for an interesting proposal to transfer some of the most attractive features of the German system to the United States. One of his specific proposals is a "2 + 2" system that combines vocational education training in the last two years of high school with two years in a technical college and work and study with a cooperating employer.

19. The Japanese offer yet another approach. As noted earlier, their educators assume that all children are equally able to learn; they do not give ability tests and conclude that those who do not succeed did not work hard enough. Relatively few Japanese youths attend vocational high schools, but they do receive extensive training when they graduate, at least if they find work in a firm that offers near "lifetime" job security.

Chapter 10: Creating Positive Incentives for Study

1. Cash payments can also be used to stimulate effort when students are administered a test that will *not* affect their grade point averages. For example,

students' performance on a National Assessment of Educational Progress examination improved in an experiment that offered them cash payments for correct answers (*Education Week*, 16 June 1993).

2. Moreover, these negative effects increase as more incentives are offered (Nicholls 1984).

3. See Doeringer and Piore 1971. Minority quotas afford a possible solution to this problem. For a variety of reasons, however, employment quotas are not popular today either with employers or with the public at large.

4. Bishop (1989b, 58) found that, under the present system, only 42 percent of black high school graduates who were not enrolled in college had found jobs four months after receiving their diplomas.

5. A new educational performance standard should be set for all students, to be met by age sixteen. This standard should be established nationally and benchmarked to the highest standard in the world. "The U.S. is the most over-tested and under-examined nation in the world. . . . As a result of this testing system, American education does not clearly reward academic effort on the part of either teachers or students" (Commission on the Skills of the American Workforce 1990, 70).

Examinations are now being developed by the National Council on Educational Standards and Testing, at the behest of the U.S. Congress.

6. See Jacobson's (1992) interesting critique of minimum competency examinations for high school graduates. He finds some negative effects on students who are above the lowest quintile of achievement.

7. See the discussion in chapter 8; and Rohlen 1983, esp. 257–58. Japanese texts indicate a heavier emphasis on Western thought. Moreover, judging from examination questions set by the more competitive Japanese universities, "the degree of detail that the better high school students must learn on such topics as Greek thought and European geography," says Rohlen, exceeds that attained by all but a very few American youths.

8. Today some writers will even apply the term *dropout* to all those who do not obtain a college degree. Its meaning has gradually been extended from those who have not completed an elementary school education to those not completing a junior high school education, to those without a high school diploma, and even to describe those not finishing college. A recent paper presented at a departmental seminar at Wayne State University used the term for those who did not complete their Ph.D. degrees.

9. The William T. Grant Foundation (1988, 131) calls for "high-quality vocational-technical education in the high schools, particularly when it is linked with post-secondary programs in community colleges and technical institutions or in quality apprenticeship programs."

10. There is a third, less direct effect: better career opportunities for those who are not successful in obtaining entrance to, or remaining in, the college preparatory program are expected to reduce the social cost of tougher standards

in these more academic programs, and this in turn undermines the argument against imposing higher academic standards.

11. Long tenures also require low quit rates by employees. The attitude of workers toward changing employers (if necessary, changing residences to do so) varies across national borders. Would a significant number of Americans reject a long tenure with the same employer, even if it offered financial incentives? (I am indebted to Philip Grossman for this point.)

12. See also Carnevale 1986; and U.S. Congress 1990. Government support for apprenticeships and on-the-job training is often recommended.

13. See the interesting article by Jean Owen (1992) on "benchmarking" practices in the private sector.

14. There is now extensive literature on school choice. Useful analyses are found in Coleman, Hoffer, and Kilgore 1981, 1982; Coons and Sugarman 1978; Keith and Page 1985; Kurth 1987; and, most recently, in the material discussed in the special December, 1992 issue of the *Economics of Education Review* and papers presented at the session on education reform at the January 1993 meetings of the Allied Social Sciences Association, especially the paper by Ballou and Podgursky (1992).

15. To deal with this last objection, advocates of reform may be expected to include quotas or targets for racial integration in their proposals. (Chubb and Moe [1990] advocate a modification of free choice which would impose racial quotas on schools.)

There is more controversy over the more general mainstreaming issue, since many feel that schools should not be required to accept a quota of students with behavioral problems, especially those with a record of violent or disruptive acts.

16. See Bachman and others 1978; Karweit 1983; and Sedlak and others 1986 for helpful discussion of the use of time in U.S. classrooms. The present requirement that public high schools in New York City distribute free condoms to children provides an extreme example.

17. As noted in chapter 8, an absence of foreign examples does mean that we lack ready models and so must be less confident of success.

18. Further research on the economics of student effort would be very useful. In a national effort students could be surveyed periodically and asked detailed questions about their use of time as well as about their own circumstances and attitudes. Linking these responses to school-based information would yield a data set that could be the basis for econometric investigations designed to provide new insights into student behavior in response to incentives.

Conclusion: Is Basic Reform Likely?

1. See Finn 1991 and Toch 1991 for recent discussions of the role of interest groups in recent educational reform efforts. See Olson 1982 for a more general discussion of the role of interest groups.

2. Mathematics standards were developed in 1989 by the National Council

of Mathematics Teachers. Standards for civics, English, the arts, geography, history, physical education, and social studies should be ready soon, and those for science, foreign languages, and economics within the next three years. The development of standards in six of these fields is subsidized by the federal government, the remainder by private funds (*Education Week*, 16 June 1993). Most recently, however, the National Educational Goals Panel was advised to omit standards for social studies, economics, and health and physical education (ibid., various issues).

3. William Bennett believes that "liberals fear that some groups will not be able to reach [meaningful] standards. . . . [T]herefore we will not have a standard, we'll have several circles. . . . We'll have a trying-hard standard, we'll have a self-esteem standard, we'll have a how-do-you-feel standard" (*Education Week*, 12 January 1994). Chester Finn says, "I fully expect we will wake up one day and have standards for home economics and driver education" (ibid., 19 January 1994).

4. See *Education Week*, various issues.

5. Standards also must not discriminate against women or racial minorities (see *Education Week*, various issues).

References

Alexander, Karl, Martha Cook, and Edward L. McDill. 1978. "Curriculum Tracking and Educational Stratification." *American Sociological Review* 43 (February): 47–66.

Alexander, Karl, and Aaron M. Pallas. 1984. "School Sector and Cognitive Performance." Johns Hopkins University Center for Social Organization of Schools, February.

Ames, Russell E., and Carole Ames, eds. 1989. *Research on Motivation in Education.* Vol. 3, *Goals and Cognitions.* San Diego: Academic Press.

——, eds. 1985. *Research on Motivation in Education.* Vol. 2, *The Classroom Milieu.* Orlando: Academic Press.

——, eds. 1984. *Research on Motivation in Education.* Vol. 1, *Student Motivation.* Orlando: Academic Press.

Anderson, Bernice, Nancy Mead, and Susan Sullivan. 1986a. "Homework: What Do National Assessment Results Tell Us?" National Assessment of Educational Progress, Princeton University, December.

——. 1986b. "Television: What Do National Assessment Results Tell Us?" National Assessment of Educational Progress, Princeton University, December.

Ascher, Carol. 1988. "High School Graduates in Entry Level Jobs: What Do Employers Want?" *Clearinghouse of Urban Education Digest,* no. 40 (February).

Bachman, Jerald G., Lloyd D. Johnston, and Patrick M. O'Malley. 1984. *Monitoring the Future: 1982 Questionnaire Responses from the Nation's High School Seniors.* Ann Arbor: Institute for Social Research.

Ballou, Dale, and Michael Podgursky. 1992. "The Structure of Pay in Private Schools: Are There Lessons for Public Schools?" MS.

Barber, Bill. 1986. "Homework Does Not Belong on the Agenda for Educational Reform." *Educational Leadership* 43 (May): 55–57.

Barron, John M., Dan A. Black, and Mark A. Loewenstein. 1989. "Job Matching and On-the-Job Training." *Journal of Labor Economics* 7 (January): 1–19.

Barton, Paul A. 1989. "Earning and Learning." Educational Testing Service, report no. 17-WL-01, March.

Beaton, Albert E. 1974. "The Influence of Education and Ability on Salary and Attitudes." In *Education, Income, and Human Behavior,* edited by F. Thomas Juster. New York: McGraw-Hill.

Becker, Gary S. 1985. "Human Capital, Effort, and the Sexual Division of Labor." *Journal of Labor Economics* 3, pt. 2 (January): S33–S58.

———. 1981. *A Treatise on the Family.* Cambridge: Harvard University Press.

———. 1975. *Human Capital,* 2d ed. New York: Columbia University Press.

———. 1965. "A Theory of the Allocation of Time." *Economic Journal* 75 (September): 493–517.

Behrman, Jere R., and Nancy Birdsall. 1983. "The Quality of Schooling: Quantity Alone Is Misleading." *American Economic Review* 73 (December): 928–46.

Behrman, Jere R., and others. 1980. *Socioeconomic Success: A Study of the Effects of Genetic Endowments, Family Environment, and Schooling.* Amsterdam: North Holland.

Bennett, William J. 1988. *Our Children and Our Country.* New York: Simon and Schuster.

Bidwell, Charles. 1965. "The School as a Formal Organization." In *Handbook of Organizations,* edited by James March. New York: Rand McNally.

Bishop, John. 1993. "Educational Reform and Technical Education?" Cornell University Working Paper no. 93.

———. 1991. "Signalling Academic Achievement to the Labor Market." Testimony before the U.S. House Labor Committee, 5 March.

———. 1989a. *Incentives for Learning: Why American High School Students Compare So Poorly to Their Counterparts Overseas.* Washington, D.C.: U.S. Department of Education.

———. 1989b. "Is the Test Score Decline Responsible for Productivity Growth Decline?" *American Economic Review* (March): 378–97.

———. 1989c. "Motivating Students to Study: Expectations, Rewards, Achievement." *National Association of Secondary School Principals Special Bulletin* 73:27–38.

———. 1989d. "The Productivity Consequences of What Is Learned in High School." *Journal of Curriculum Studies* 22 (March–April): 101–26.

———. 1987. "The Recognition and Reward of Employee Performance." *Journal of Labor Economics* 5, pt. 2 (October): S36–S56.

Blackburn, McKinley L., David E. Bloom, and Richard B. Freeman. 1990. "The Declining Economic Position of Less Skilled American Men." In *A Future of Lousy Jobs?* edited by Gary Burtless. Washington, D.C.: Brookings Institution.

Blakemore, Arthur E., and Stuart Low. 1983. "A Simultaneous Determination of Post–High School Education Choice and Labor Supply." *Quarterly Review of Economics and Business* 23:81–92.

Blaug, Mark. 1985. "Where Are We Now in the Economics of Education?" *Economics of Education Review* 4:17–28.

Blits, Jan H., and Linda S. Gottfredson. 1990. "Employment Testing and Job Performance." *Public Interest* 98:18–25.

Boissiere, M., J. B. Knight, and R. H. Sabot. 1985. "Earnings, Schooling, Ability, and Cognitive Skills." *American Economic Review* 75 (December): 1016–30.

Bound, John, Zvi Griliches, and Bronwyn H. Hall. 1986. "Wages, Schooling, and IQ of Brothers and Sisters: Do the Family Factors Differ?" *International Economic Review* 27 (February): 77–105.

Bowles, Samuel. 1977. "The Production Process in a Competitive Economy." *American Economic Review* 75 (March): 16–36.

Bowles, Samuel, and Herbert Gintis. 1976. *Schooling in Capitalist America.* New York: Basic Books.

Boyer, Ernest L. 1983. *High School: A Report on Secondary Education in America.* New York: Harper and Row.

Boyett, Joseph H., and Henry P. Conn. 1991. *Workplace 2000: The Revolution Reshaping American Business.* New York: Dutton.

Brookover, Wilbur, and others. 1979. *School Systems and Student Achievement* New York: Praeger.

Brown, Byron W. 1992. "Why Governments Run Schools." *Economics of Education Review* 11 (December): 287–300.

Brown, Byron W., and Daniel H. Saks. 1987. "The Microeconomics of the Allocation of Teachers' Time and Student Learning." *Economics of Education Review* 6:319–32.

———. 1981. "The Microeconomics of Schooling." *Review of Research in Education* 9:209–54.

———. 1980. "Production Technologies and Resource Allocations within Classrooms and Schools." In *The Analysis of Educational Productivity,* edited by R. Dreeben and J. A. Thomas. Cambridge, Mass: Ballinger.

———. 1975. "The Production and Distribution of Cognitive Skills within Schools." *Journal of Political Economy* 83 (June): 571–93.

Bryan, William R. 1988. "The Value of a College Education." *Illinois Business Review* 45 (October): 3–7.

Buis, Ann Gibson. 1953. "An Historical Study of the Role of the Federal Government in the Financial Support of Education, with Particular Reference to Legislative Proposals and Action." Ph.D. diss., Ohio State University.

Callahan, Raymond. 1962. *Education and the Cult of Efficiency.* Chicago: University of Chicago Press.

Camber, L. C., and John Keeves. 1973. *Science Achievement in Nineteen Countries.* New York: Wiley.

Campbell, Joseph. 1959. *The Masks of God: Primitive Mythology.* New York: Viking.

Card, David, and Alan Krueger. 1990. "Does School Quality Matter? Returns to Education and the Characteristics of Public Schools in the United States." Working Paper no. 3358. National Bureau of Economic Research, Cambridge, Mass.

Carnevale, Anthony P. 1986. "The Learning Enterprise." *Training and Development Journal* 40 (January): 18–26.

Carnoy, Martin, and Henry M. Levin. 1985. *Schooling and Work in the Democratic State.* Stanford: Stanford University Press.

Carroll, J. B. 1963. "A Model for School Learning." *Teachers College Record* 64 (May): 723–33.

Carson, C. C., R. M. Huelskamp, and T. D. Woodall. 1993. "Perspectives on Education in America: An Annotated Briefing." *Journal of Educational Research* 86, no. 5 (May–June).

Catterall, James S. 1992. "Theory and Practice of Family Choice in Education: Taking Stock—Review Essay." *Economics of Education Review* 11 (December): 407–16.

Chamberlain, Gary, and Zvi Griliches. 1977. "More on Brothers." In *Kinometrics: Determinants of Socioeconomic Success within and between Families,* edited by P. J. Taubman. Amsterdam: North Holland.

Chiswick, Barry R. 1988. "Differences in Education and Earnings across Racial and Ethnic Groups: Tastes, Discrimination, and Investments in Child Quality." *Quarterly Journal of Economics* 103 (August): 571–97.

Chubb, John, and Terry M. Moe. 1990. *Politics, Markets, and America's Schools.* Washington, D.C.: Brookings Institution.

Clark, Reginald. 1983. *Family Life and School Achievement: Why Poor Black Children Succeed or Fail.* Chicago: University of Chicago Press.

Clune, William, with Paula White and Janice Patterson. 1989. *The Implementation and Effects of High School Graduation Requirements: First Steps toward Curricular Reform.* New Brunswick, N.J.: Center for Policy Research in Education, Rutgers University.

Cohany, Sharon R. 1986. "What Happened to the High School Class of 1985?" *Monthly Labor Review* 109, no. 10 (October): 28–30.

Cohen, David K., and Richard J. Murnane. 1985. "The Merits of Merit Pay." *Public Interest* 80:3–30.

Cohen, Michael. 1983. "Instructional, Management, and Social Conditions in Effective Schools." In *School Finance and School Improvement,* edited by Allan Odden and L. Dean Webb. Cambridge, Mass.: Ballinger.

Coleman, James, Thomas Hoffer, and Sally Kilgore. 1982. *High School Achievement: Public, Catholic, and Private Schools Compared.* New York: Basic Books.

———. 1981. *Public and Private Schools: An Analysis of High School and Beyond.* Chicago: NORC.

Coleman, James, and others. 1966. *Equality of Educational Opportunity.* Washington, D.C.: Department of Health, Education, and Welfare.

Commission on the Skills of the American Workforce. 1990. *America's Choice: High Skills or Low Wages?* Rochester, N.Y.: National Center on Education and the Economy.

Condry, John. 1978. "The Role of Incentives in Socialization." In *The Hidden Costs of Reward: New Perspectives on the Psychology of Human Motivation,* edited by Mark R. Lepper and David Greene. New York: Wiley.

Condry, John, and James Chambers. 1978. "Intrinsic Motivation and the Process of Learning." In *The Hidden Costs of Reward: New Perspectives on the Psychology of Human Motivation,* edited by Mark R. Lepper and David Greene. New York: Wiley.

Coons, John, and Stephen Sugarman. 1978. *Education by Choice: The Case for Family Control.* Berkeley: University of California Press.

Covington, Martin V. 1984. "The Motive for Self-Worth." In *Research on Motivation in Education.* Vol. 1, *Student Motivation,* edited by Russell E. Ames and Carole Ames. Orlando: Academic Press.

Crain, Robert. 1984. "The Quality of American High School Graduates: What Personnel Officers Say and Do about It." Johns Hopkins Center for Social Organization of Schools, report no. 354, May.

Cremin, Lawrence. 1962. *The Transformation of the School.* New York: Knopf.

Csikszentmihalyi, Mihaly, and Reed Larson. 1984. *Being Adolescent: Conflict and Growth in the Teenage Years.* New York: Basic Books.

Cubberley, Ellwood. 1920. *The History of Education.* Boston: Houghton Mifflin.

Cusick, Philip A. 1983. *The Egalitarian Ideal and the American High School.* New York: Longmans.

Deci, Edward L. 1975. *Intrinsic Motivation.* New York: Plenum.

Denison, Edward F. 1962. *The Sources of Economic Growth in the United States and the Alternatives before Us.* New York: Committee for Economic Development.

DiPrete, Thomas A., and others. 1987. *Discipline and Order in American High Schools.* Chicago: National Center for Educational Statistics.

Doeringer, Peter, and Michael Piore. 1971. *Internal Labor Markets and Manpower Training.* Lexington, Mass.: Heath Lexington.

Dooley, Martin, and Peter Gottschalk. 1985. "The Increasing Proportion of Men with Low Earnings in the United States." *Demography* 22 (February): 25–34.

Doyle, Denis P., and Terry W. Hartle. 1985. *Excellence in Education: The States Take Charge.* Washington, D.C.: American Enterprise Institute for Public Policy Research.

Duckworth, Kenneth. 1983. "Some Ideas about Student Cognition, Motivation, and Work." Report to the National Commission on Excellence in Education, Washington, D.C.

Eaton, Jonathan, and Harvey S. Rosen. 1980. "Taxation, Human Capital, and Uncertainty." *American Economic Review* 70 (September): 705–15.

Eberts, Randall W., and Joe A. Stone. 1988. "Student Achievement in Public Schools: Do Principals Make a Difference?" *Economics of Education Review* 11, no. 3: 291–99.

Education Week. Various issues.

Edwards. Richard. 1976. "Individual Traits and Organizational Incentives: What Makes a 'Good' Worker?" *Journal of Human Resources* 11, no. 1: 51–68.

Ekstrom, Ruth B., and others. 1986. "Who Drops Out of High School and Why? Findings from a National Study." *Teachers College Record* 87:356–73.

Ellwood, David T. 1982. "Teenage Unemployment: Permanent Scars or Temporary Blemishes?" In *The Youth Labor Market Problem: Its Nature, Causes, and Consequences,* edited by Richard Freeman and David Wise. Chicago: University of Chicago Press.

Epstein, Joyce. 1988. "The Homework Practices, Achievements, and Behaviors of Elementary School Students." Johns Hopkins University Center for Research on Elementary and Middle Schools, report no. 26, July.

European Foundation for the Improvement of Living and Working Conditions. 1988. *The Changing Face of Work: Researching and Debating the Issues.* Luxembourg: European Communities Official Publications Office.

Farrar, Eleanor. 1983. "Review of Effective Schools Programs." In *Effective Schools Programs in High Schools: Implications for Policy, Practice, and Research,* edited by Eleanor Farrar and others. Washington, D.C.: National Commission on Excellence in Education.

Fetters, William B. 1975. *National Longitudinal Study of High School Class of 1972.* Department of Health, Education and Welfare, National Center for Educational Statistics. Washington, D.C.: USGPO.

Fetters, William B., George H. Brown, and Jeffrey A. Owings. 1984. "High School Seniors: A Comparative Study of the Classes of 1972 and 1980. High School and Beyond, a National Longitudinal Study for the 1980s." Department of Health, Education and Welfare. National Center for Educational Statistics. Washington, D.C.: USGPO.

Finn, Chester E. 1991. *We Must Take Charge: Our Schools and Our Future.* New York: Free Press.

Firestone, William, Susan H. Fuhrman, and Michael Kirst. 1989. *The Progress of Reform: An Appraisal of State Education Initiatives.* Rutgers University, Center for Policy Research in Education, Research report ser. RR-014, October.

Frederick, C. W., and H. J. Walberg. 1980. "Learning as a Function of Time." *Journal of Educational Research* 73 (March–April): 183–194.

Freeman, Richard B. 1975. "Overinvestment in College Training?" *Journal of Human Resources* 10:287–311.

Gamoran, Adam. 1987. "The Stratification of High School Learning Opportunities." *Sociology of Education* 60 (July): 135–55.

Garen, John E. 1988. "Empirical Studies of the Job Matching Hypothesis." *Research in Labor Economics* 9:187–224.

George, Rosemary. 1987. "Youth Policies and Programs in Selected Countries: Youth and America's Future." Report of the William T. Grant Foundation Commission on Work, Family and Citizenship, Washington, D.C., August.

Ghez, Gilbert, and Gary S. Becker. 1975. *The Allocation of Time and Goods over the Life Cycle.* New York: National Bureau of Economic Research.

Gintis, Herbert. 1969. "Alienation and Power: Towards a Radical Welfare Economics." Ph.D. diss., Harvard University.

Goodlad, John. 1984. *A Place Called School: Prospects for the Future.* New York: McGraw-Hill.

Gordon, David M., Richard Edwards, and Michael Reich. 1982. *Segmented Work, Divided Workers.* New York: Cambridge University Press.

Gottfredson, Linda S. 1993. "Clinton's New Form of Race-Norming." *Wall Street Journal.* Editorial, 3 June.

————. 1984. "The Role of Intelligence and Education in the Division of Labor." Johns Hopkins University Center for Social Organization of Schools, report no. 355, February.

Grant, William T., Foundation. Commission on Work, Family, and Citizenship. 1988. *The Forgotten Half: Pathways to Success for America's Youth and Young Families.* Washington, D.C.: William T. Grant Foundation.

Graves, Frank Pierrepont. 1971. *Great Educators of Three Centuries.* New York: AMS Press.

Greenberger, Ellen, and Laurence Steinberg. 1986. *When Teenagers Work.* New York: Basic Books.

Griliches, Zvi, and William M. Mason. 1972. "Education, Income and Ability." *Journal of Political Economy* 80 (May–June): S74–S103.

Hamilton, Stephen F. 1990. *Apprenticeship for Adulthood: Preparing Youth for the Future.* New York: Free Press.

Hanson, E. Mark. 1979. *Educational Administration and Organizational Behavior.* Boston: Allyn and Bacon.

Hanson, Sandra L., and Alan L. Ginsburg. 1985. "Gaining Ground: Values and High School Success." Washington, D.C.: Decision Resources Corporation.

Hanushek, Eric A. 1992. "Making Policy When You Don't Know the Production Process." Working paper.

————. 1986. "The Economics of Schooling: Production and Efficiency in Public Schools." *Journal of Economic Literature* 24 (September): 1147–77.

Hause, John C. 1974. "Ability and Schooling as Determinants of Lifetime Earnings, or If You're So Smart Why Aren't You Rich?" In *Education, Income and Human Behavior,* edited by F. Thomas Juster. New York: McGraw-Hill.

————. 1972. "Earnings Profile: Ability and Schooling." *Journal of Political Economy* 80, pt. 2 (May–June): S108–S138.

Hauser, Robert M., and Thomas N. Daymont. 1977. "Schooling, Ability and Earnings: Cross-Sectional Findings Eight to Fourteen Years after High School Graduation." *Sociology of Education* 50 (July): 182–206.

Haveman, Robert H., and Barbara L. Wolfe. 1984. "Schooling and Economic Well-Being: The Role of Nonmarket Effects." *Journal of Human Resources* 19:377–407.

Heckman, James, and Solomon Polachek. 1974. "Empirical Evidence on the Functional Form of the Earnings-Schooling Relationship." *Journal of the American Statistical Association* 69 (June): 350–54.

Hersch, Joni, and Patricia Reagan. 1990. "Job Match, Tenure and Wages Paid by Firms." *Economic Inquiry* 28 (July): 488–509.

Heyns, Barbara, and Sophia Catsambis. 1986. "Mother's Employment and Children's Achievement: A Critique." *Sociology of Education* 59 (July): 140–51.

Hirsch, E. D. 1987. *Cultural Literacy: What Every American Needs to Know.* Boston: Houghton Mifflin.

Hirschman, Albert O. 1982. *Shifting Involvements, Private Interest and Public Action.* Princeton, N.J.: Princeton University Press.

———. 1970. *Exit, Voice and Loyalty.* Cambridge, Mass.: Harvard University Press.

Hirschorn, Michael W. (Grant Foundation Commission on Youth and America's Future). 1988. "Harsh Prospects Are Seen for Americans Who Do Not Attend College." *Chronicle of Higher Education* 31 (27 January): A35.

Hollingshead, August B. 1949. *Elmtown's Youth.* New York: Wiley.

Holsinger, Donald B. 1982. "Time, Content and Expectations as Predictors of School Achievement in the USA and Other Developed Countries: A Review of IEA Evidence." Report to the National Commission on Excellence in Education, Washington, D.C., September.

Howe, Harold, II. 1990. "Thinking about Our Children and Youth: The Forgotten Half?" *Community Education Journal,* 4–10.

Hurn, Christopher J., and Barbara Burn. 1983. "An Analytical Comparison of Educational Systems: Overview of Purposes, Policies and Outcomes." Report to the National Commission on Excellence in Education, Washington, D.C.

Husen, Torsten. 1982. "A Cross-National Perspective on Assessing the Quality of Learning." Report to the National Commission on Excellence in Education, Washington, D.C.

———, ed. 1967. *International Study of Achievement in Mathematics.* New York: Wiley.

Inkeles, Alex. 1979. "National Differences in Scholastic Performance." *Comparative Education Review* 23 (October): 386–407.

International Assessment for the Evaluation of Educational Achievement. 1988. *Science Achievement in Seventeen Countries: A Preliminary Report.* Oxford: Pergamon Press.

Jablonski, Mary, Larry Rosenblum, and Kent Kinze. 1988. "Productivity, Age, and Labor Composition Changes in the United States." *Monthly Labor Review* 111 (September): 34–38.

Jackson, Philip W. 1968. *Life in Classrooms.* New York: Holt, Rinehart and Winston.

Jacobson, Jonathan E. 1992. "Mandatory Testing Requirements and Pupil Achievement." Working paper.

Jencks, Christopher, and others. 1979. *Who Gets Ahead? The Determinants of Economic Success in America.* New York: Basic Books.

———. 1972. *Inequality: A Reassessment of the Effect of Family and Schooling in America.* New York: Basic Books.

Johnson, Thomas. 1978. "Time in School: The Case of the Prudent Patron." *American Economic Review* 68 (December): 862–72.

Jones, Ethel B., and John D. Jackson. 1990. "College Grades and Labor Market Rewards." *Journal of Human Resources* 75:253–66.

Jorgenson, Dale W. 1987. *The Contribution of Education to U.S. Economic Growth.* Cambridge, Mass.: Harvard University Press.

Junge, Denis A., and others. 1983. "Perceptions of Business and Industry: Basic Skills Necessary for Successful Employment Compared to Competency Levels of Entry Level Employees." Illinois State Board of Education, June.

Karweit, Nancy. 1983. *Time on Task: A Research Review,* rev. ed. Report to the National Commission on Excellence in Education, Washington, D.C.

Katz, Lawrence, and Kevin Murphy. 1992. "Changes in Relative Wages, 1963–1987: Supply and Demand Factors." *Quarterly Journal of Economics* 107 (February): 35–78.

Katz, Michael. 1971. *Class, Bureaucracy, and Schools.* New York: Praeger.

Kean, Thomas H. 1988. *The Politics of Inclusion.* New York: Free Press.

Kearns, David, and Denis Doyle. 1988. *Winning the Brain Race.* San Francisco: Institute for Contemporary Studies Press.

Keith, Timothy Z. 1982. "Time Spent on Homework and High School Grades: A Large-Sample Path Analysis." *Journal of Educational Psychology* 74 (April): 248–53.

Keith, Timothy Z., and Ellis B. Page. 1985. "Do Catholic High Schools Improve Minority Student Achievement?" *American Educational Research Journal* 22:337–49.

Keith, Timothy Z., and others. 1986. "Parental Involvement, Homework, and TV Time: Direct and Indirect Effects on High School Achievement." *Journal of Educational Psychology* 78 (October): 373–80.

Killingsworth, Mark. 1983. *Labor Supply.* New York: Cambridge University Press.

King, Edmund J. 1967. *Other Schools and Ours,* 3d ed. New York: Holt, Rinehart and Winston.

Kodde, David. 1988. "Unemployment Expectations and Human Capital Formation." *European Economic Review* 32 (October): 1615–30.

———. 1986. "Uncertainty and the Demand for Education." *Review of Economics and Statistics* 68 (August): 460–67.

Kolstad, Andrew. 1982. "Does College Pay? Wage Rates before and after Leaving School." *NCES Bulletin* (National Center for Education Statistics).

Kooreman, Peter, and Arie Kapteyn. 1990. "On the Empirical Implementation of Some Game Theoretic Models of Household Labor Supply." *Journal of Human Resources* 25:584–98.

Koretz, Daniel, and others. 1992. *National Educational Standards and Testing: A Response to the Recommendations of the National Council on Education Standards and Testing.* Santa Monica, Calif.: Rand Corporation.

Kramer, Martin. 1989. "Empty Chairs: What Happens to Students Who Don't Go to College?" *Change* 21 (January–February): 6–7.

Krein, Sheila F. 1986. "Growing Up in a Single Parent Family: The Effect on Education and Earnings of Young Men." *Family Relations* 35 (January): 161–68.

Kurth, Michael M. 1988. "Teachers, Unions and Excellence in Education: An Analysis of the Decline in SAT Scores. Reply." *Journal of Labor Research* (Fall): 389–94.

———. 1987. "Teachers, Unions and Excellence in Education: An Analysis of the Decline in SAT Scores." *Journal of Labor Research* (Fall): 351–67.

Layard, Richard, and G. Psacharopoulos. 1974. "The Screening Hypothesis and the Returns to Education." *Journal of Political Economy* 82 (September–October): 985–98.

Lazear, Edward. 1981. "Agency, Earnings Profiles, Productivity, and Hours Restriction." *American Economic Review* 71 (September): 605–20.

———. 1977a. "Academic Achievement and Job Performance." *American Economic Review* 67 (March): 252–54.

———. 1977b. "Education: Consumption or Production?" *Journal of Political Economy* 85 (June): 569–97.

LeCompte, Margaret Diane, and Anthony Gary Dworkin. 1991. *Giving Up on School: Student Dropouts and Teacher Burnouts.* Newbury Park, Calif.: Corwin Press.

Lee, Valerie E., and Anthony S. Bryk. 1988. "Curriculum Tracking as Mediating the Social Distribution of High School Achievement." *Sociology of Education* 61 (April): 78–94.

Lepper, Mark R., and David Greene. 1978. *The Hidden Cost of Reward: New Perspectives on the Psychology of Human Motivation.* New York: Wiley.

Levin, Henry M. 1992. "Market Approaches to Education: Vouchers and School Choice." *Economics of Education Review* 11 (December): 279–85.

———. 1972. *The Cost to the Nation of Inadequate Education.* U.S. Senate. Select Committee on Equal Opportunity. Washington, D.C.: USGPO.

Levin, Henry M., and Mun C. Tsang. 1987. "The Economics of Student Time." *Economics of Education Review* 6:357–64.

Lewin-Epstein, Noah. 1981. "Youth Employment during High School—An Analysis of High School and Beyond: A National Longitudinal Study for the Eighties." National Center for Educational Statistics. Chicago: National Opinion Research Center.

Lewis, Anne C. 1988. "Barriers in the Path of the Non–College Bound." *Phi Delta Kappan* 68 (February): 396–97.

Lieberman, Myron. 1989. *Privatization and Educational Choice*. New York: St. Martin's Press.

———. 1980. *Public Sector Bargaining: A Policy Reappraisal*. Lexington, Mass.: Lexington Books.

Link, Charles R., and James G. Mulligan. 1986. "The Merits of a Longer School Day." *Economics of Education Review* 5:373–81.

Lisack, J. P., and Kevin D. Shell. 1988. *Labor Force Study: Elkhart, Indiana*. Lafayette, Ind.: Purdue University Office of Manpower Studies.

Liu, Pak-Wai. 1986. "Human Capital, Job Matching and Earnings Growth between Jobs: An Empirical Analysis." *Applied Economics* (U.K.) 18 (October): 1135–47.

Lockwood, Ben. 1986. "Transferable Skills, Job Matching, and the Inefficiency of the 'Natural' Rate of Unemployment." *Economic Journal* 96 (December): 961–74.

McCall, Brian P. 1990. "Occupational Matching: A Test of Sorts." *Journal of Political Economy* 98 (February): 45–69.

McElroy, Marjorie B. 1990. "The Empirical Content of Nash-Bargained Household Behavior." *Journal of Human Resources* 25:559–83.

McGraw, Kenneth O. 1978. "The Detrimental Effects of Reward on Performance: A Literature Review and Prediction Model." In *The Hidden Costs of Reward: New Perspectives on the Psychology of Human Motivation*, edited by Mark R. Lepper and David Greene. New York: Wiley.

McPartland, James, and Edward L. McDill. 1977. *Violence in Schools*. Lexington, Mass.: Lexington Books.

McPartland, James, and others. 1986. "The School's Role in the Transition from Education to Work." Johns Hopkins University Center for Social Organization of Schools, report no. 362.

Manski, Charles F. 1992. "Educational Choice (Vouchers) and Social Mobility." *Economics of Education Review* 11 (December): 351–69.

———. 1989. "Schooling as Experimentation: A Reappraisal of the Post Secondary Dropout Phenomenon." *Economics of Education Review* 8: 305–12.

Markey, James. 1988. "The Labor Market Problems of Today's High School Dropouts." *Monthly Labor Review* 111 (June): 36–43.

Mathios, Alan D. 1989. "Education, Variation in Earnings, and Nonmonetary Compensation." *Journal of Human Resources* 24:456–68.

Meyer, Adolphe E. 1967. *An Educational History of the American People*, 2d ed. New York: McGraw-Hill.

Meyer, John, W. Richard Scott, and David Strang. 1987. "Centralization, Fragmentation, and School District Complexity." *Administrative Science Quarterly* 32 (June): 186–201.

Meyer, Robert, and David Wise. 1982. "High School Preparation and Early Labor Force Experience." In *The Youth Labor Market Problem: Its Nature, Causes, and Consequences,* edited by Robert Freeman and David Wise. Chicago: University of Chicago Press.

Michael, Robert. 1973. "Education in Non-Market Production." *Journal of Political Economy* 81 (March–April): S128–S164.

Miguel, Richard J., and Robert C. Faulk. 1984. "Youth's Perception of Employer Standards and Effects on Employment Outcomes and Employer Evaluation." Ohio State University.

Miller, Paul W. 1989. "Low Wage Youth Employment: A Permanent or Transitory State?" *Economic Record* (June): 126–36.

Milne, Ann M., and others. 1986. "Single Parents, Working Mothers, and the Educational Achievement of School Children." *Sociology of Education* 59 (July): 125–39.

Mincer, Jacob. 1984. "Over-Education or Under-Education?" In *Education and Economic Productivity,* edited by Edwin Dean. Cambridge, Mass.: Ballinger.

Moffitt, Robert A. 1987. "Symposium on the Econometric Evaluation of Manpower Training Programs: Introduction." *Journal of Human Resources* 22:149–56.

———. 1979. "The Labor Supply Response in the Gary Experiment." *Journal of Human Resources* 14:477–87.

Morris, Van Cleve, and others. 1984. *Principles in Action: The Reality of Managing Schools.* Columbus, Ohio: C. E. Merrill.

Mortensen, Dale T. 1988. "Wages, Separations, and Job Tenure: On-the-Job Specific Training or Matching?" *Journal of Labor Economics* 6 (October): 445–71.

Mulligan, J. 1984. "A Classroom Production Function." *Economic Inquiry* 22 (April): 218–26.

Murray, Charles, and R. J. Herrnstein. 1992. "What's Really behind the SAT Score Decline?" *Public Interest,* no. 106 (Winter): 32–56.

Musgrave, Richard A. 1984. *The Theory of Public Finance.* New York: McGraw-Hill.

Myers, David, and others. 1987. "Student Discipline and High School Performance." *Sociology of Education* 60 (January): 18–33.

National Association of Secondary School Principals. 1985. *How Fares the Ninth Grade? A Day in the Life of a Ninth Grade.* Reston, Va.: National Association of Secondary School Principals.

National Center for Educational Statistics. 1990. "National Education Goals: Options for Measuring Student Achievement." Washington, D.C.: National Center for Educational Statistics.

———. 1984. "High School and Beyond: A National Longitudinal Study for the 1980s. Two Year Results: The Status of 1980 Sophomores." Washington, D.C.: National Center for Educational Statistics.

National Center on Education and the Economy. 1990. *America's Choice: High Skills or Low Wages? The Report of the Commission on the Skills of the American Workforce*. Rochester, N.Y.: National Center on Education and the Economy.

National Commission on Excellence in Education. 1983. *A Nation at Risk*. Washington, D.C.: U.S. Department of Education.

National Commission on Testing and Public Policy. 1990. *From Gatekeeper to Gateway: Transforming Testing in America*. Chestnut Hill, Mass.: Boston College.

National Education Association. 1987. "Extending the School Day and School Year." Washington, D.C.: National Education Association.

Natriello, Gary, ed. 1987. *School Dropouts: Patterns and Policies*. New York: Teachers College Press.

Natriello, Gary, and Edward L. McDill. 1986. "Performance Standards, Student Effort on Homework, and Academic Achievement." *Sociology of Education* 59 (January): 18–31.

Nelson, E. Howard, and Jewell L. Gould. 1988. "Teachers, Unions and Excellence in Education: An Analysis of the Decline in SAT Scores. Comment." *Journal of Labor Research* (Fall): 379–87.

Neufeld, Barbara, and others. 1983. "A Review of Effective Schools Research: The Message for Secondary Schools." Report to the National Commission on Excellence in Education. Washington, D.C.: National Commission on Excellence in Education.

Nicholls, John G. 1984. "Concepts of Ability and Achievement Motivation." In *Research on Motivation in Education*. Vol. 1, *Student Motivation*, edited by Russell E. Ames and Carole Ames. Orlando: Academic Press.

Nolfi, George J. 1978. *Experiences of Recent High School Graduates: The Transition to Work or Postsecondary Education*. Lexington, Mass.: Lexington Books.

Nothdurft, William. 1989. *School Works: Reinventing Public Schools to Create the Workforce of the Future*. Washington, D.C.: Brookings Institution.

Olnek, Jay, and Paul Taubman, ed. 1977. *Kinometrics: The Determinants of Socioeconomic Success within and between Families*. Amsterdam: North Holland.

Olson, Mancur. 1982. *The Rise and Decline of Nations: Economic Growth, Stagflation and Social Rigidities*. New Haven, Conn.: Yale University Press.

Orazem, Peter F., and J. Peter Mattila. 1986. "Occupational Entry and Uncertainty: Males Leaving High School." *Review of Economics and Statistics* 68 (May): 265–73.

Owen, Jean V. 1992. "Benchmarking World-Class Manufacturing." *Manufacturing Engineering* 108, no. 3 (March): 29–34.

Owen, John D. 1989. *Reduced Working Hours*. Baltimore: Johns Hopkins University Press.

——. 1986. *Working Lives*. Lexington, Mass.: D. C. Heath.

——. 1979. *Working Hours*. Lexington, Mass.: D. C. Heath.

——. 1975. *School Inequality and the Welfare State*. Baltimore: Johns Hopkins University Press.

——. 1969. *The Price of Leisure*. Rotterdam: Rotterdam University Press.

Pace, C. Robert. 1983. "Achievement and the Quality of Student Effort." Report to the National Commission on Excellence in Education, Washington, D.C.

Paschal, Rosanne A., Thomas Weinstein, and Herbert J. Walberg. 1984. "The Effects of Homework on Learning: A Quantitative Synthesis." *Journal of Educational Research* 78 (November–December): 97–104.

Peng, Samuel S., and others. 1982. "Effective High Schools: What Are Their Attributes?" Paper presented at the annual meeting of the American Psychological Association, Washington, D.C., 23–27 August.

Powell, Arthur, Eleanor Farrar, and David Cohen. 1985. *The Shopping Mall High School*. Boston: Houghton Mifflin.

Purkey, Stewart C., and Marshall S. Smith. 1983. "Effective Schools: A Review." *Elementary School Journal* 83 (March): 427–52.

Raffini, James P. 1988. *Student Apathy: The Protection of Self-Worth*. Washington, D.C.: National Education Association.

Ravitch, Diane. 1983. *The Troubled Crusade*. New York: Basic Books.

——. 1974. *The Great School Wars*. New York: Basic Books.

Ravitch, Diane, and Chester E. Finn, Jr. 1987. *What Do Our Seventeen-Year-Olds Know?* New York: Harper and Row.

Resnick, Daniel P., and Lauren B. Resnick. 1985. "Standards, Curriculum, and Performance: A Historical and Comparative Perspective." *Educational Researcher* 14 (April): 5–20.

Rock, Donald A., and others. 1985. "Factors Associated with Decline of Test Scores of High School Seniors, 1972–1980." Princeton, N.J.: Educational Testing Service.

Rohlen, Thomas P. 1983. *Japan's High Schools*. Berkeley: University of California Press.

Rohling, Thomas A. 1986. "Screening and Human Capital Theory: An Empirical Test." *Industrial Relations* (Canada) 41 (December): 817–26.

Rosenbaum, James E., and Takshiko Kariya. 1989. "From High School to Work: Market and Institutional Mechanisms in Japan." *American Journal of Sociology* 94 (May): 1334–65.

Rothman, Robert. 1990. "S.A.T. Verbal Scores Continue Slide to Lowest Level since 1980 and 1981." *Education Week* (5 September): 7.

Rumberger, Russel W. 1983. "The Influence of Family Background on Education, Earnings, and Wealth." *Social Forces* 61 (March): 755–73.

————. 1981. *Overeducation in the U.S. Labor Market.* New York: Praeger.

————. 1980. "The Economic Decline of College Graduates: Fact or Fallacy?" *Journal of Human Resources* 15:99–111.

Rutter, Michael. 1983. "School Effects on Pupil Progress: Research Findings and Policy Implications." *Child Development* 54 (February): 1–29.

Rutter, Michael, and others. 1979. *Fifteen Thousand Hours: Secondary Schools and Their Effects on Children.* Cambridge: Harvard University Press.

Schmidt, R. M. 1983. "Who Maximizes What? A Study in Student Time Allocation." *American Economic Review* 73 (May): 23–28.

Sedlak, Michael W., and others. 1986. *Selling Students Short: Classroom Bargains and Academic Reform in the American High School.* New York: Teachers College Press.

Sewell, William H., and Robert M. Hauser. 1975. *Education, Occupation and Earnings: Achievement in the Early Career.* New York: Academic Press.

Shanahan, Timothy, and Herbert J. Walberg. 1985. "Productive Influences on High School Achievement." *Journal of Educational Research* 78 (July–August): 357–63.

Shank, Susan. 1986. "Preferred Hours of Work and Corresponding Earnings." *Monthly Labor Review* 109 (November): 40–44.

Shapiro, C., and J. E. Stiglitz. 1984. "Equilibrium Unemployment as a Worker Discipline Device." *American Economic Review* 74 (June): 433–44.

Sizer, Theodore R. 1984. *Horace's Compromise: The Dilemma of the American High School.* Boston: Houghton Mifflin.

Skinner, B. F. 1976. *Walden Two.* New York: Macmillan.

Smelser, Neil J. 1989. "Self-Esteem and Social Problems: An Introduction." In *The Social Importance of Self-Esteem,* edited by Andrew Mecca, Neil J. Smelser, and John Vasconcellos. Berkeley: University of California Press.

Snow, Richard E. 1982. "Intelligence, Motivation, and Academic Work." Report to the National Commission on Excellence in Education. Washington, D.C.: National Commission on Excellence in Education.

Spence, A. M. 1974. "Job Market Signalling." *Quarterly Journal of Economics* 7 (March): 296–332.

Stafford, Frank P., and Greg J. Duncan. 1985. "The Use of Time and Technology by Households in the United States." In *Time, Goods, and Well-Being,* edited by F. Thomas Juster and Frank P. Stafford. Ann Arbor: Institute for Social Research.

Stallings, J. 1980. "Allocated Academic Learning Time Revisited; or, Beyond Time on Task." *Educational Researcher* 9 (December): 11–16.

Stevenson, Harold W. 1986. "Classroom Behavior and Achievement of Japanese, Chinese, and American Children." In *Child Development and Education in Japan,* edited by Hiroshi Azuma, Kenji Hakata, and Harold W. Stevenson. New York: Freeman Press.

Stevenson, Harold W., and Shin-ying Lee. 1990. *Contexts of Achievement.*

Monographs of the Society for Research in Child Development, ser. no. 221, vol. 55, nos. 1–2.

Stevenson, Harold W., and James W. Stigler. 1992. *The Learning Gap: Why Our Schools Are Failing and What We Can Learn from Japanese Education.* New York: Summit Books.

Stiglitz, Joseph E. 1975. "The Theory of 'Screening,' Education and the Distribution of Income." *American Economic Review* 65 (June): 283–300.

Stipek, Deborah. 1984. "The Development of Achievement Motivation." In *Research on Motivation in Education.* Vol. 1, *Student Motivation,* edited by Russell E. Ames and Carole Ames. Orlando: Academic Press.

Sum, Andrew, Paul Harrington, and Paul Simpson. 1985. "Educational Attainment, Academic Ability, and Employability: Planning and Design of a Youth Program." *Thrust: The Journal for Employment and Training Professionals* 6 (January–February): 1–22.

Summers, Anita A., and Barbara L. Wolfe. 1977. "Do Schools Make a Difference?" *American Economic Review* 67 (September): 639–53.

Task Force on Teaching as a Profession. 1986. *A Nation Prepared: Teachers for the Twenty-first Century.* Washington, D.C.: Carnegie Forum on Education and the Economy.

Taubman, Paul, and Terence Wales. 1974a. "Education as Investment and Screening Device." In *Education, Income, and Human Behavior,* edited by F. Thomas Juster. New York: McGraw-Hill.

———. 1974b. "Mental Ability and Higher Educational Attainment in the Twentieth Century." In *Education, Income, and Human Behavior,* edited by F. Thomas Juster. New York: McGraw-Hill.

Thurow, Lester. 1975. *Generating Inequality: Methods of Distribution in the U.S. Economy.* New York: Basic Books.

Toch, Thomas. 1991. *In the Name of Excellence.* New York: Oxford University Press.

Todd, Helen M. 1913. "Why Children Work: The Children's Answer." *McClure's* 40 (April): 68–79.

Tsang, Mun C. 1987. "The Impact of Underutilization of Education on Productivity: A Case Study of the U.S. Bell Companies." *Economics of Education Review* 6:239–54.

Tsang, Mun C., and Henry M. Levin. 1985. "The Economics of Overeducation." *Economics of Education Review* 4:93–104.

Tyack, David. 1974. *The One Best System: A History of American Urban Education.* Cambridge, Mass.: Harvard University Press.

Uchitelle, Louis. 1990. "Surplus of College Graduates Dims Job Outlook for Others." *New York Times,* 18 June.

U.S. Congress. Office of Technology Assessment. 1990. *Worker Training: Competing in the New International Economy.* Washington, D.C.: USGPO.

U.S. Department of Education. 1991a. *America 2000: An Education Strategy.* Washington, D.C.: USGPO.

———. 1991b. *Digest of Educational Statistics.* Washington, D.C.: USGPO.

Verdugo, Richard R., and Naomi T. Verdugo. 1989. "The Impact of Surplus Schooling on Earnings: Some Additional Findings." *Journal of Human Resources* 24:629–43.

Wachtel, Paul. 1974. "The Returns to Investment in Higher Education: Another View." In *Education, Income, and Human Behavior,* edited by F. Thomas Juster. New York: McGraw-Hill.

Walberg, Herbert J. 1985. "Homework's Powerful Effects on Learning." *Educational Leadership* 42 (April): 76–79.

Walberg, Herbert J., Rosanne A. Paschal, and Thomas Weinstein. 1986. "Effective Schools Use Homework Effectively: Reply." *Educational Leadership* 43 (May): 58.

Warswick, G. D. N., ed. 1985. *Education and Economic Performance.* National Institute of Economic and Social Research, Policy Studies Institute, and Royal Institute of International Affairs Joint Studies in Public Policy Series no. 9. Aldershot, Eng., and Brookfield, Vt.: Gower.

Wehlage, Gary G., and Robert A. Rutter. 1986. "Dropping Out: What Do Schools Contribute to the Problem?" *Teachers College Record* 87:374–92.

Weick, Karl. 1976. "Educational Organizations as Loosely Coupled Systems." *Administrative Science Quarterly* 21 (March): 1–19.

Weiner, Bernard. 1984. "Principles for a Theory of Student Motivation and Their Application within an Attributional Framework." In *Research on Motivation in Education.* Vol. 1, *Student Motivation,* edited by Russell E. Ames and Carole Ames. Orlando: Academic Press.

Weisbrod, Bertram A. 1964. *External Benefits of Public Education.* Princeton University report, Industrial Relations section, ser. no. 105.

Weiss, Andrew. 1988. "High School Graduation, Performance, and Wages." *Journal of Political Economy* 96 (August): 785–820.

Welch, Finis. 1973. "Black-White Differences in Returns to Schooling." *American Economic Review* 63 (December): 892–907.

West, Edwin G. 1992. "Autonomy in School Provision: Meanings and Implications—Review Essay." *Economics of Education Review* 11 (December): 417–25.

White, Merry. 1987. *The Japanese Educational Challenge.* New York: Free Press.

Williamson, Oliver E. 1980. "The Organization of Work." *Journal of Economic Behavior and Organization* 1:5–38.

Williamson, Oliver E., Michael L. Wachter, and Jeffrey E. Harris. 1975. "Understanding the Employment Relation: The Analysis of Idiosyncratic Exchange." *Bell Journal of Economics* 6:250–78.

Willis, Robert J., and Sherwin Rosen. 1979. "Education and Self-Selection." *Journal of Political Economy* 87, pt. 2 (October): S7–S36.

Wirt, Frederick, and Michael Kirst. 1982. *Schools in Conflict: The Politics of Education.* Berkeley: McCutchan.

Wise, David A. 1979. *Academic Achievement and Job Performance: Earnings and Promotions.* New York: Garland.

———. 1975. "Academic Achievement and Job Performance." *American Economic Review* 65 (June): 360–66.

Wise, David A., and Robert Meyer. 1984. "The Transition from School to Work: The Experiences of Blacks and Whites." *Research in Labor Economics* 6:123–76.

Wolpin, Kenneth. 1977. "Education and Screening." *American Economic Review* 67 (December): 949–58.

Yang, Bijou, David Lester, and Jeri-Lynn Gatto. 1989. "Working Students and Their Course Performance: An Extension to High School Students." *Psychological Reports* 64 (February): 218.

Zigler, Edward F. 1989. "Addressing the Nation's Child Care Crisis: The School of the Twenty-first Century." *American Journal of Orthopsychiatry* 59 (October): 484–91.

Zimiles, Herbert. 1982. "The Changing American Child: The Perspective of Educators." Report to the National Commission on Excellence in Education, Washington, D.C., October.

Index

ability, innate, emphasis on, 9, 12–13, 97
accident victims, 4
achievement: changes over time, 6; effect on future earnings, 40–47, 63–64, 102n; effect on productivity, 9, 63–64; international comparisons of, 5; low levels a concern to employers, 44
aerobics classes, 4
affirmative action, 42
Aid to Families with Dependent Children, 107n
alcoholics, recovery programs for, 4
Alexander, Karl, 106n, 113
Ames, Carole, 97n, 113, 125, 128, 129
Ames, Russell E., 97n, 113, 125, 128, 129
Anderson, Bernice, 96n, 113
apprentices, 69, 78–79, 85–86
Ascher, Carol, 102n, 113
Azuma, Hiroshi, 127

Bachman, Jerald G., 26, 95n, 98n, 110n, 113
backward-sloping supply curve of labor, 18
Ballou, Dale, 110n, 113
Barber, Bill, 95n, 113
Barron, John M., 102n, 113
Barton, Paul A., 101n, 113
Beaton, Albert E., 101n, 113
Becker, Gary S., 22, 27, 28, 33, 99n, 101n, 107n, 114, 119
Behrman, Jere R., 101n, 114
Bennett, William J., 111n, 114
Bidwell, Charles, 9n, 56n, 114
Birdsall, Nancy, 101n, 114
Bishop, John, 38, 40, 41, 42, 44, 63, 96n, 101n, 102n, 109n, 114
Black, Dan A., 102n, 113
Blackburn, McKinley L., 101n, 114
Blakemore, Arthur E., 114
Blaug, Mark, 100n, 101n, 114
Blits, Jan H., 114

Bloom, David E., 114
boarding schools, 36–37
Boissiere, M., 101n, 115
Bound, John, 101n, 115
Bowles, Samuel, 96n, 107n, 115
Boyer, Ernest L., 103n, 115
Boyett, Joseph, 87n, 115
Brookover, Wilbur, 115
Brown, Byron, 89, 103n, 115
Brown, George H., 6, 102n, 118
Bryan, William R., 101n, 115
Bryk, Anthony S., 106n, 122
Buis, Ann Gibson, 105n, 115
bureaucracy in schools, 23–24, 51, 52, 53–54, 85
Burn, Barbara, 120
Burtless, Gary, 114
Bush, George, 92
business community: opposition to federal aid to education, 105n; support for education reform, 63

Callahan, Raymond, 104n, 115
Camber, L. C., 95n, 115
Campbell, Joseph, 98n, 115
Card, David, 101n, 102n, 115
Carnevale, Anthony P., 110n, 116
Carnoy, Martin, 96n, 116
Carroll, J. B., 103n, 116
Carson, C. C., 116
cash payments to students, 80–81, 108n
Catholic schools, 103n
Catsambis, Sophia, 120
Catterall, James S., 89, 116
Chamberlain, Gary, 102n, 116
Chambers, James, 81, 117
child labor laws, 25
Chiswick, Barry R., 101n, 116
Chubb, John, 53, 88, 103n, 110n, 116
Clark, Reginald, 106n, 116
classroom contracts, 49–50
Clinton, William, 92

Greene, David, 81, 117, 122, 123
Griliches, Zvi, 101n, 102n, 115, 116, 119
Grossman, Philip, 110n

Hakata, Kenji, 127
Hall, Bronwyn H., 101n, 115
Hamilton, Stephen F., 108n, 119
Hanson, E. Mark, 49, 50, 52, 103n, 119
Hanson, Sandra L., 119
Hanushek, Eric A., 5, 102n, 104n, 119
Harrington, Paul, 128
Harris, Jeffrey E., 129
Hartle, Terry W., 117
Hause, John C., 101n, 119
Hauser, Robert M., 101n, 102n, 119, 127
Haveman, Robert H., 104n, 120
Hawthorne experiments, 49
Heckman, James, 101n, 120
Herrnstein, R. J., 6, 38, 96n, 124
Hersch, Joni, 102n, 120
Heyns, Barbara, 120
higher culture, 14, 55, 104n, 109n
higher education, x, 38–39, 60, 64, 70, 79, 95n
Hirsch, E. D., 106n, 120
Hirschman, Albert O., 48, 72, 120
Hirschorn, Michael W., 101n, 120
Hoffer, Thomas, 110n, 116
Hollingshead, August B., 25, 120
Holsinger, Donald B., 95n, 102n, 120
homework, 3, 5, 6, 8, 15, 20, 21, 22, 37, 40, 50, 67, 70, 72, 80, 95n
Howe, Harold II, 120
Huck Finn, 13
Huelskamp, R. M., 116
human capital theory, 33–34, 45, 60, 69, 70, 100n
Hurn, Christopher J., 120
Husen, Torsten, 95n, 120

income maintenance programs, x, 19, 74, 107n
information flows between schools and employers, 20, 35–37, 41–42, 46–47, 54, 56, 69, 70, 82–83, 90, 93
Inkeles, Alex, 95n, 120
internal labor market, 60
International Assessment for the Evaluation of Educational Achievement, 95n, 120
international competition, 5, 60, 63, 68, 71

Jablonski, Mary, 105n, 120
Jackson, John D., 102n, 121
Jackson, Philip W., 121
Jacobson, Jonathan E., 109n, 121
Japanese students, 5, 6, 12, 67–70, 85, 97n, 98n, 106n, 108n, 109n; commuting to school, 6
Jencks, Christopher, 101n, 121
job interview, importance of, 43
Johnson, Thomas, 95n, 121
Johnston, Lloyd D., 26, 95n, 113n
Jones, Ethel B., 102n, 121
Jorgenson, Dale W., 105n, 121
Junge, Denis A., 121
Juster, F. Thomas, 113, 119, 127, 128, 129

Kapteyn, Arie, 20, 122
Kariya, Takshiko, 106n, 126
Karweit, Nancy, 95n, 110n, 121
Katz, Lawrence, 101n, 121
Katz, Michael, 97n, 121
Kean, Thomas H., 121
Kearns, David, 4, 95n, 107n, 121
Keeves, John, 95n, 115
Keith, Timothy Z., 95n, 110n, 121
Kilgore, Sally, 110n, 116
Killingsworth, Mark, 121
King, Edmund J., 13, 67, 68, 69, 70, 106n, 121
Kinze, Kent, 105n, 120
Kirst, Michael, 101n, 103n, 108n, 118, 130
Knight, J. B., 101n, 115
Kodde, David, 101n, 121
Kolstad, Andrew, 101n, 122
Kooreman, Peter, 20, 122
Koretz, Daniel, 122
Kramer, Martin, 102n, 122
Krein, Sheila F., 122
Krueger, Alan, 101n, 102n, 115
Kurth, Michael M., 96n, 103n, 110n, 122

labor leisure choice, 17–18, 23
labor market, changes in, 5–7, 37, 38, 86–87, 94n, 101n
labor supply theory, ix, x, 17–20
Larson, Reed, 8, 96n, 97n, 98n, 117
Latin, 3, 36, 82
Layard, Richard, 100n, 122
Lazear, Edward, 101n, 107n, 122

Pace, C. Robert, 126
Page, Ellis B., 110n, 121
Pallas, Aaron M., 106n, 113
parental influence, 22, 53–55, 88, 99
part-time jobs: attitudes toward, 14–15,
    26–27, 98n; changing nature of, 25–
    26; demand for, in inner city, 25,
    100n; growth in employer demand,
    24–25; as source of entry-level posi-
    tions, 26; time spent in, 14–15, 26
Paschal, Rosanne A., 95n, 126, 129
Patterson, Janice, 116
Peng, Samuel S., 103n, 126
Piore, Michael, 60, 109n, 117
Podgursky, Michael, 110n, 113
Polachek, Solomon, 101n, 120
Powell, Arthur, 103n, 126
principals, 49, 51, 52, 53, 88
private schools, 53–55, 88, 89, 103n
Protestant work ethic, 12
Psacharopoulos, G., 100n, 122
psychology, x, 9–10, 108n
Purkey, Stewart C., 103n, 126

Raffini, James P., 10, 126
Ravitch, Diane, 104n, 106n, 126
Reagan, Patricia, 102n, 120
Reich, Michael, 60, 119
Resnick, Daniel P., 83, 126
Resnick, Lauren B., 83, 126
retirements, x, 19
Rock, Donald A., 96n, 126
Rohlen, Thomas P., 6, 68, 70, 98n, 106n,
    109n, 126
Rohling, Thomas A., 100n, 126
Rosen, Harvey S., 117
Rosen, Sherwin, 101n, 130
Rosenbaum, James E., 106n, 126
Rosenblum, Larry, 105n, 120
Rothman, Robert, 96n, 126
Rumberger, Russel W., 105n, 106n, 126
Rutter, Michael, 103n, 127
Rutter, Robert A., 76, 107n, 129

Sabot, R. H., 101n, 115
Saks, Daniel H., 103n, 115
Schmidt, R. M., 95n, 127
school day and year, length of, 3, 5, 13,
    70, 72, 91
Scott, W. Richard, 103n, 123
screening theory, 34–37, 43–44, 60, 64

Sedlak, Michael W., 6, 15, 33, 34, 35, 46,
    49, 50, 59, 95n, 98n, 100n, 103n, 107n,
    108n, 110n, 127
self-esteem, 9–11, 86, 97n, 108n, 109n
Sewell, William H., 102n, 127
Shanahan, Timothy, 95n, 127
Shank, Susan, 23, 127
Shapiro, C., 107n, 127
Shell, Kevin D., 43, 123, 146
shirking, 21, 22, 46–47, 49, 51, 99n
Simpson, Paul, 128
Sizer, Theodore R., 103n, 127
skills boards, 93–94
Skinner, B. F., 81, 127
Smelser, 97n, 127
Smith, Marshall S., 103n, 126
Snow, Richard E., 127
socialization, 8–9, 12, 33–34, 43, 46, 64,
    65, 100n, 104n
social objective function, 73–74
sociology, x
Spence, A. M., 100n, 127
spending time with friends, 14
sports, 14
Sputnik, 59, 92
Stafford, Frank P., 99n, 127
Stallings, J., 95n, 127
Steinberg, Laurence, 15, 26, 98n, 119
Stevenson, Harold W., 95n, 127, 128
Stigler, James W., 128
Stiglitz, Joseph E., 100n, 107n, 127, 128
Stipek, Deborah, 97n, 128
Stone, Joe A., 101n, 117
Strang, David, 103n, 123
student reaction function, 73–74
study effort: cost of, 18–19, 64–65, 66;
    effect of affluence on, 18, 19; effect on
    academic achievement, ix, 4–5; effect
    on future income, 17, 19–20, 37, 38–
    39, 40, 55, 82; long-term trends in, 6;
    national attitudes toward, 12–14, 59–
    60, 73, 97n; student attitudes toward,
    8–11, 55, 97n, 108n
Sugarman, Stephen, 110n, 117
Sullivan, Susan, 96n, 113
Sum, Andrew, 128
Summers, Anita A., 102n, 128
summer vacations, 5

Taubman, Paul, 101n, 125, 128
taxpayers, 65–66, 74, 105n, 107n
tax revenues, 62

Library of Congress Cataloging-in-Publication Data

Owen, John D.
    Why our kids don't study : an economist's
perspective / John D. Owen.
        p.   cm.
    Includes bibliographical references (p.   ) and
index.
    ISBN 0-8018-4925-x (alk. paper)
        1. Academic achievement—United States.
    2. Study environment—United States.
    3. Motivation in education—United States.
    4. Labor supply, Effect of education on—United
States.   I. Title.
    LB1062.6.O94   1995
    371.8'1—dc20   94-21829